THE RESULT OF FAILED LEADERSHIP

THE RESULT OF FAILED LEADERSHIP

THE REPUBLIC OF LIBERIA
1943-2003

Tuoquellie Garlon Niagawoe

THE CRIES OF A TERRIFIED LIBERIA: EYEWITNESS REPORTS OF THE HORRORS COMMITTED BY THE DOE'S GOVERNMENT SOLDERS AND THE REBELLION FORCES.

AT MIDNIGHT. ON APRIL 12, 1980, SEVENTHTEEN ENLISTED MEN IN THE COVER OF THE NIGHT SEIZED THE GOVERNMENT OF THE LATE PRESIDENT WILLIAM RICHARD TOLBERT JR. AT MIDNIGHT, ON DECEMBER 24, 1989, REBEL TROOPS STORMED ACROSS THE LIBERIAN BORDER; COLLAPSING THE GOVERNMENT OF THE LATE MASTER SERGEANT SAMUEL KAYAN DOE IN A MATTER OF (8) MONTHS AND NINE DAYS. THE BRUTALITY WITH WHICH THIS ILLEGAL INVASION WAS CARRIED OUT AND THE SENSELESS BARBARIC ATROCITIES TO WHICH LIBERIAN POPULATION ARE SUBJECT ON A DAILY BASIS-WILL SHOCK THE ENTIRE WORLD.

TUOQUELLIE GARELON NIAGAWOE III WAS IN LIBERIA AT THE VERY STARTING AND TOWARDS ITS ANTICIPATED END OF THE CIVIL WAR. TRAVELED TO THE NEIGHBORING COUNTRY-IVORY COAST UNTO THE UNITED STATES OF NORTH AMERICA. CONTINUES INVASION AND ITS AFTER-MATH FROM STUNNED AND ANGRY REFUGEES OR JOURNALIST. FROM EXILED, DISPLACED OR DISLOCATED MEMBERS OF THE RULING FAMILY AND PARTY, RESISTANCE FIGHTERS, MEDICAL PROFESSIONALS, WIVES, AND MOTHERS, SHE HEARD STARTING TALES OF TERROR: INFANTS TORN FROM INCUBATORS, AND LEFT TO DIE ON HOSPITAL FLOORS. NURSES AND DOCTORS GUN DOWN BEFORE PATIENTS EYES UNTHOUGHTFULLY, WOMEN RAPED SAVAGELY. ESCAPEES AND REFUGEES WERE SHOT IN THE BACK OF THE HEAD AS THEY ATTEMPTED TO ESCAPE THROUGH THE BUSHES.

THE DEMON OF LIBERIA PRESENTS THESE EYEWITNESS STORIES TO ME WHICH BRING TO LIGHT FOR THE FIRST

TIME THE EXTENT OF THE CRIMES COMMITTED AGAINST THE NATION'S CIVILIANS POPULATION. A SHOCKING INDICTMENT OF THE "TAYLOR, REBEL FORCES," THIS BOOK WILL INCREASE WORLD'S TRUE NOTION OF SAMUEL KAYAN DOE AND CHARLES G. TAYLOR AND RAISE THE FRIGHTENING QUESTION OF THEY INTENT TO DO NEXT AFTER THE COUP AND CIVIL WAR IF, HE (SAMUEL DOE) WAS ELECTED AND CHARLES TAYLOR WAS ELECTED AFTER THE CIVIL WAR; DEFEATED IN THE SO-CALLED GENERAL ELECTIONS OF 1997? THE ANSWER TO THIS QUESTION REST IN THE HEARTS OF LIBERIANS.

To order additional copies of this book, contact:
Xlibris
1-888-795-4274
www.Xlibris.com
Orders@Xlibris.com
586863

CONTENTS

THE RESULTS
OF FAILED LEADERSHIP

When a leadership fails, these are some of the tools it uses against humanity and their results.

1. INTIMIDATION
2. HARASSMENT
3. FALSE IMPRISONMENT
4. COUP D'ETAT
5. CIVIL-CRISIS
6. FALSE-ALRAM
7. FALSE-HEARTED
8. FALSE-HOOD
9. National Recession
10. Economics down turn

These things happen when the leader notices that his or her time is running out and has done nothing. When the leadership finds out that he has not live up to the campaign promises, he starts false-alarming the nation. Intimidation is an easy act failing leadership turn to always. Plays blame game with his opponents. Tells the citizens he would have done his best if his political opponents were not bothering him. Particularly, in Africa, the leadership becomes very aggressive and cruel. He sends out his loyalists to smell his opponents.

Falsified reports are often brought back to him against peaceful, loyal, innocent taxpayers who try to look up for the middle-class citizens. Of course, this is what he really expects of his so-called loyalists. He terminates those whom he claims are against his administration. Street, bar, barbershop, beauty salon and of course at the work place, his loyalists seek information to feed him with. He lives on this information for cover-ups. Now, the question comes, how long will he do this? People get tied of sort leadership and seek a different avenue of survival.

The Results of Failed Leadership.

I am pleased to make known to the world how leadership failure has had serious burden on the entire nation of Liberia and others inclusive. When a leadership realizes that it is heading to failure it becomes very cohesive and aggressive. I have listed some of the characters of doomed leadership.

Let's take a look at the religious leadership for a moment. When the Church of England began to mix politics with religion, failure popped up. The leadership became confused and defused in operation. Religious sacrament was misapplied, sold for money, infallibility preached throughout the church. Today is of no exception. The Christian church is confused again, and again. The marketing of the "Gospel Ministry," has started again. The church leadership is doom to fail whenever we begin to see these things popping up the religious setting.

Church Leaders are making mockery out of Christianity everywhere again; the political leadership is not involved in this today. Rather the church leaders are mixing up politics with the sacrament. The reason is simple, these failed political leaders who are covering up their failures with the word of God. Somebody will argue that it has happened before. Yes, it did happen in the case of Saul of Assure who became known as Brother Paul. But I want you to know that does thing for a reason and at a specific time and place. Everybody will not be used as Saul was; so please watch your steps.

It is inexcusable for any religious leader to use Paul's experience as an excuse for misusing the religious power of the church. Such leadership is banned to fail. The people of God are confused today by the unacceptable behaviors leadership in the very church of God. Failed political leaders are moving into the churches for cover ups. In this respect, Christian leadership must watch for these failures coming. God has tasked them with leadership of His children and they have failed their Creator-God. They are coming with their personal rules and regulations into the church of God to confuse its leadership. Remember, these are the same people who have confused society with their numerous rules and zero techniques. Instead of these folks learning from their mistakes, they want the Church of God leadership to copy their failed techniques.

I am very much hampered by these unacceptable attitudes as I travel visiting other churches. Marriage is a blessed sacrament of God in its entirety, but it is been disregarded abused by these failures of society. Spiritually, these are society outcast.

Our African brothers and sisters in the Americas and Europe, need to understand that God allowed their parents to be brought into those places mentioned for the safety and serving of those later running to them away from tyranny. With all these information and others, today, Liberia still remains free as it was met by the slave-traders. Our brothers and sisters' children only return home up to presence to meet their descendants; these descendants have all the right to return to Africa freely as they want and own properties as they choice to. This nation-Liberia should have been an independent nation if, the so-called friendly world power did not come to rob her of its mineral resources which are the gifts of life from our supreme Being-God the Creator; thus, making her an independence nation today. I must admit that it is sad for one nation to take away the gifts of God from other nations and survives on them and leave them in needy poverty life with the intention of enslaving them to her and nobody says anything. One may rightfully say, the world power survive on the poor nations and call them, "developing nations." They do not recognize the fact that they are the causative agent of the disease which has paralyzed the continent of Africa and other parts of the world. Isn't it a fact when keenly observed, these so-called world powers are the developing nations of the world? Why do I say this, because they are always looking into all other parts of the world picking up natural resources that they do not have to help them develop from other countries to help them? If truly you are a developed, world power nation, what are you looking for in those countries that you consider under-develop. Why not stay home? Clearly, the behaviors of those whom we consider world power, are the world poorest. They do not have anything to make them powerful unless we who are called world poor nations give it to them. Perfect examples are; Liberia with the iron ore, rubber, diamonds and gold, Sierra Leone with its land of diamond and gold and Ghana which is known for gold and also called the coast of Africa, Congo Brazzaville and Congo Leopuville(Zaire) which are known to be the heart of Africa; the list goes on and on. Many years ago, David Livingstone and Henry Stanley met in this region of Africa, it became historically known as the heart of Africa because of its riches. Today, our so-called world power has stolen so much worth from these areas until they shamefully named them poor countries. My question to these world power nations is who made these countries poor nations? All world power nations please stand before the mirror and you will be able to identify the people who make these nations poor nations. I link this behavior to the behavior of the slave-masters who refused the slaves to have connections with their homeland when they forcefully made them slaves and took them into a strange land with their faces tied and eyes closed not knowing where they were going. Today, the slave-masters have become losers because the faces of the slave-descendants are no more tied neither eyes closed. If, any one decides to remain a slave, he or she is responsible for being a slave. God has removed the black cloth from the faces of black slaves from Africa and opens their eyes to see everything that was in hiding from them. Such thing as education which is the most important point of information to clear the minds of people, was hidden from black history tells us. Today, we have great black doctors of philosophy, medicines, theology and etc. It sadden my heart to see some black folks who have decided to keep their hearts in slavery and continue using the slave mentality of fear of masters, laziness, complaining, and moreover, hatred against the ambitious strong ones. If the black people will take their minds out of slavery and place into human freedom with the understanding that every freedom has some responsibilities attached, it will work well with them. Let them travel in the world freely and see the other side of the globe, compare and contrast, you will be able to make a sound decision. God did not limit the movement and power of any human being during His creation process. God used these words, saying, "Let man have dominion over the whole earth." This is why God continues to use human being through whom He does His wondrous for the human family. However, it is sad that man could limit himself and others with the use of political ideology to hinder the progress of others with senseless ideas from his little negative, weak and wicked, heart.

Too many of us the children of Africa, particularly Liberia, do fairly understand that the supper power is the problem, not the developing countries. If they the supper power would just leave the developing nations along and stop taking away their God given rights of their natural resources, they will survive. But the leadership role playing in those so-called developing nations have always been dominated by the supper power by using their political magnifying glass to see and destabilize the peace and stability of those countries. This world power can only see the

Evil committed in those little nations and capitalize on them; but not the good plans implemented by the leadership.

The News Media

The Media is been used by the so called "World Power" to dig out only the evil-darts of those parts of the world and burry the ones in their back yard; of course, God has revealed to us all. We can see hungry children digging in dump stock looking for food, dying with diseases, naked people looking for clothes and they cannot find in the back yard of those supper powers; yet we not hear any see these things in the news. Media's work should be transparent, not translucent. If the media decides to support cover ups, then the institution loses its true meaning and also disappoints society.

This book might sound political, but it is more spiritual than political. At no time in history God ever happily allowed His children to be ruled by wicked king. Though they might be stubborn, but He loves them. We as servants of God cannot be silent about these unacceptable behaviors of society. God has given us responsibility to carry out in this world; that is speaking the truth, regardless of the situation. Stand up and speak out, you are a child of a "Great King."

Leadership

Leadership has been described as the, "process of social influence in which one person can enlist the aid support of others in the accomplishment of a common task." However, in other parts of the world, leadership is been described as, selfish-gain, cruel-treatment, harassment, intimidation, and inhumane behavior. The theories of leadership will be discussed from here on.

Theories of Leadership

We shall compare and contrast the styles and theories of leadership geographically, historically and traditionally. The theory of leadership can be accepted in other areas whereas other parts of the world couldn't be accepted based on tradition, culture and history. Let's take a keen look at the West African nation-Liberia's history of leadership; Liberia was originally ruled by tribal kings and queens.

These governments were Aristocratic or Autocratic led by dictatorial leadership. Tradition was strongly observed and respected by all. Those who went against such leadership were put to death. Getting a leader out of such so-called government, one must also remember that these unacceptable behavior which have been the norm of sort society, will possibly be done away. The individual born and raised in this society has already inhabited some traditional-cultural attitudes from former leaders. In order to bring up a genuine leadership from such community, we must uneducated and re-educate any product from such society to become a good leader.

Taking the children of those leaders without a genuine, constructive and integrated leadership education, is a wasting of time and taxpayers money. I will call it ill-repeated effects which benefit no one.

Trait Theory

This theory tries to describe the types of behavior and personality tendencies associated with effective leadership. Perhaps, this is the first academic theory of leadership. Thomas Carlyle (1841) can be considered one of the pioneers of the trait theory, using such approach to identify the talents, skills and physical characteristics of men who arose to power.

The passed records of leadership in Liberia, to be specific, needs to dig into its passed leadership records for they are mixed. Let's first take a look at the entrance, from 1664, when the Dutch man name Pedro de Sentry entered into this part of Africa naming it "The Green Coast," later calling its name now, "Liber" now call Liberia.

This Portuguese trader saw this particular region of Africa as a free area. Liber means free in latin. I cannot understand why Liberians are

Celebrating Independence Day when their country was never colonized by any great power. What I would like to make clear to all Liberians and friends of Liberia is, we did not get our independence from any country. Rather we declared to the free world that we exist. This is far different from gaining independence from your former colonial slave's masters. I want the world to know from this book that Liberia did not declare her independence from anybody at any time in history.

Of course, you may want to talk about our African brothers and sisters who were taken into slavery by enemies against their will and pleasure, and then later returned home into their own homeland of nativity. This was not freedom as you may call it. It was God's way of relief for His children who have suffered under the cruel hands of enemies. Therefore it doesn't give anyone the right to say Liberia declares her independence from any country. Even though, some parts of history says that the United States Government was forced by the King of England to buy a home for the freed-slaves of North America which Liberia became the answer. This part of history is incorrect. The little place which was given to the returning brothers and sisters which I called them could not have become a nation as one might be made to think. It is the political of others to divide and rule. In order to set the returning brothers and sisters against their home brothers and sisters as the custom is, the enemies used these words, "the love of liberty brought us here." Not to mention, it was the same love of liberty that made their parents slaves into a foreign land for many years. I strongly believe that those who brought back the so-called freed African slaves should have said these are the offspring of your brothers and sisters whom were stolen from you, now we believe that they should come and inherit their parents God given gifts of inheritance. Today, just as the Jews and the Egyptians live together in peace, so it is with Europeans, Americans and Africans doing the same. Somebody was cruelly forced into slavery under the cruel hands of the others before, but this is how the Creator decided to unify the human race. God allowed little Joseph to go into slavery into Egypt to safe and serve his father and brothers from the great famine everywhere. The results of failed leadership are dangerous and unacceptable in today's world. Yester-years, leaders were free to make as much mistakes as they wish. People were afraid to speak out for fear of been send to jail or executed. Human life was of no value, meaningless to prospective failed leadership. A story is told of a district paramount chief from Bong County, Liberia, West Africa. This chief made human sacrifice at the beginning of every new moon for the twenty-seven unbroken years he was in power.

Anyone can imagine the number of innocent souls this maid man sent into their graves during his twenty-seven years regime. This brutal, barbaric leadership of course is band to fail. God has never blessed a leadership of this type. God creates or appoints leaders; self-made leadership cannot or will never succeed. Whenever God appoints or creates a leader, He provides him or her wisdom and knowledge and moreover, divine security protection.

Let us look in the book of Jeremiah the prophet; chapter 1, where God appointed Jeremiah for the nation of Israel as a prophet to tell the nation the truth. He promised Jeremiah that He would be with him all the way through and told him, "do not be afraid of their faces." The Lord knew that it was not going to be for the elders of Israel to accept message of their wrong doing from a young child like Jeremiah. Therefore Jeremiah's life was placed in danger always. History indicates that no good preacher of God life has being of any value to people in this world. The same was with Joshua, the son of nun. God told him to be strong and be courageous. The war of the Gospel comes from within. A perfect example would be the betraying of our Lord Jesus Christ, no body from the outside betrayed him, but somebody from within. Judas decides to get rid of Jesus Christ when he (Judas) got to know Christ well. So our war in the church comes from within the church. Those, whom we are ordained and consecrated to preach the eternal Gospel to, are the same that can crucify us, not those that are out there. The downfall of every administration comes from within. Many leaders of the world of yester-years and today are often misled by their so-called loyalists. Do not feed them with the truth, but lies; thus, causing their lives and ending their administration in disastrous. It should be incumbent on all people who love a leader to tell him or her truth of any wrong doing. Generally, it has been a failure and disappointment on the part of people who claim to be friend of a leader to not tell him or her truth of their wrong doing. We might think that it is human being whom sets up leadership, no, it is God who appoints and sets up leadership and brings down the other. When the King of Babylon-Nebuchadnezzar's thought that he brought himself into power and did whatever he did, God called him a fool, because King Nebuchadnezzar did not do anything good with the use of his personal knowledge without the involvement of God. In my life as an African preacher, I have come to find out that too leaderships do not recognize God as their commander-in-chief; but these leaderships have always failed. Those Israelite leaders who made God their direct commander-in-chief and kept in close link/contact with God, thou they made some errors, yet, God was always and moreover, He spare them.

Whatever you will read about in this book was cause by failed leadership. Now, we are moving to a very particular topic what I call; "Leadership Model for Developing Countries." We shall embark on this topic very highly. Looking at the errors of leadership today and yester-years.

False-imprisonment

This is one aspect of a failed leadership in Africa which usually lead to coup'de'tate or civil-war. Political opponents are often arrested and sent to jail without court trial.

False-imprisonment becomes the norm of his community. People are often accused and send into jail for crime they never committed. Employees are often fire for what they class as administrative reason. In every work place, there is what I call chiefs but no Indians. Everybody tries to become chief/boss. Arbitrary arrest is common everywhere. The results of failed leadership are dangerous and unacceptable in today's world. Yester-years, leaders were free to make as much mistakes as they wish. People were afraid to speak out for fear of been send to jail or executed. Human life was of no value, meaningless to prospective failed leadership. A story is told of a district paramount chief from Bong County, Liberia, West Africa. This chief made human sacrifice at the beginning of every new moon for the twenty-seven unbroken years he was in power.

Anyone can imagine the number of innocent souls this maid man sent into their graves during his twenty-seven years regime. This brutal, barbaric leadership of course is band to fail. God has never blessed a leadership of this type. God creates or appoints leaders; self-made leadership cannot or will never succeed. Whenever God appoints or creates a leader, He provides him or her wisdom and knowledge and moreover, divine security protection.

Whatever you will read about in this book was cause by failed leadership. Now, we are moving to a very particular topic what I call; "Leadership Model for Developing Countries." We shall embark on this topic very highly. Looking at the passed records of leadership in Liberia, to be specific, needs to dig into its passed leadership records for they are mixed. Let's first take a look at the entrance, from 1664, when the Dutch man name Pedro de Sentry entered into this part of Africa naming it "The Green Coast," later calling its name now, "Liber" now call Liberia.

This Portuguese trader saw this particular region of Africa as a free area. Liber means free in latin. I cannot understand why Liberians are celebrating Independence Day when their country was colonized by any great power. What I would like to make clear to all Liberians and friends of Liberia is, we did not get our independence from any country. Rather we declared to the free world that we exist. This is far different from gaining independence from your former colonial slave's masters. I want the world know from this book that Liberia did not her independence from nobody at any time in history.

Of course, you may want to talk about our African brothers and sisters who were taken into slavery by enemies against their will and pleasure, and then later returned home into their own land of nativity. This was not freedom as you may call it. It was God's way of relief for His children who have suffered under the cruel hands of enemies. Therefore it doesn't give anyone the right to say Liberia declares her independence from any country. Today, just as the Jews and the Egyptians live together in peace, so it is with Europeans, Americans and Africans doing the same. Somebody was cruelly forced into slavery under the cruel hands of the others before, but this is how the Creator decided to unify the human race. God allowed little Joseph to go into slavery into Egypt to safe and serve his father and brothers from the great famine.

Our African brothers and sisters in the Americas and Europe, need to understand that God allowed their parents to be brought into those places mentioned for the safety and serving of those later running to them away tyranny. With all these information and others, today, Liberia still remains free as it was met by the slave-traders. Our brothers and sisters' children only return home up to presence. These descendants have all the right to return to Africa freely as they want and own properties as they choice to. This nation-Liberia should have been an independent nation if so-called friendly world power did not come to rob her of its mineral resources thus, making her an independence nation today.

Too many of us the children of Africa, particularly Liberia, do fairly understand that the supper power is the problem, not the developing countries. If they the supper power would just leave the developing nations along and stop taking away their God given rights of their natural resources, they will survive. But the leadership role playing in those so-called developing nations have always been dominated by the supper power by using their political magnifying glass to see and destabilize the peace and stability of those countries. This world power can only see the evil committed in those little nations and capitalize on them; but not the good plans implemented by the leadership.

The News Media

The Media is been used by the so called "World Power" to dig out only the evil-darts of those parts of the world and burry the ones in their back yard; of course, God has revealed to us all. We can see hungry children digging in dump stock looking for food, dying with diseases, naked people looking for clothes and they cannot find in the back yard of those supper powers; yet we not hear any see these things in the news. Media's work should be transparent, not translucent. If the media decides to support cover ups, then the institution loses its true meaning and also disappoints society.

This book might sound political, but it is more spiritual than political. At no time in history God ever happily allowed His children to be ruled by wicked king. Though they might be stubborn, but He loves them. We as servants of God cannot be silent about these unacceptable behaviors of society. God has given us responsibility to carry out in this world; that is speaking the truth, regardless of the situation. Stand up and speak out, you are a child of a "Great King."

Leadership

Leadership has been described as the, "process of social influence in which one person can enlist the aid support of others in the accomplishment of a common task." However, in other parts of the world, leadership is been described as, selfish-gain, cruel-treatment, harassment, intimidation, and inhumane behavior. The theories of leadership will be discussed from here on.

Theories of Leadership

We shall compare and contrast the styles and theories of leadership geographically, historically and traditionally. The theory of leadership can be accepted in other areas whereas other parts of the world couldn't be accepted based on tradition, culture and history. Let's take a keen look at the West African nation-Liberia's history of leadership; Liberia was originally ruled by tribal kings and queens. These governments were Aristocratic or Autocratic led by dictatorial leadership. Tradition was strongly observed and respected by all. Those who went against such leadership were put to death. Getting a leader out of such so-called government, one must also remember that these unacceptable behavior which have been the norm of sort society, will possibly be done away. The individual born and raised in this society has already inhabited some traditional-cultural attitudes from former leaders. In order to bring up a genuine leadership from such community, we must uneducated and reeducate any product from such society to become a good leader.

Taking the children of those leaders without a genuine, constructive and integrated leadership education, is a wasting of time and taxpayers money. I will call it ill-repeated effects which benefit no one.

Trait Theory

This theory tries to describe the types of behavior and personality tendencies associated with effective leadership. Perhaps, this is the first academic theory of leadership. Thomas Carlyle (1841) can be considered one of the pioneers of the trait theory, using such approach to identify the talents, skills and physical characteristics of men who arose to power.

ON
PRINCE
NESS
loody Liberia

The latest struggle for power in Liberia has turned what was already a violent country into one where atrocities are as common as flies feeding on murdered Monrovian civilians. For more on the tribes involved, their principal players and everyday life in the country, see "Flashpoint Liberia" in SOF's October 1990 issue.

"**C**OMMANDO!" the half-crazed adolescent guard shrieked in my face. I had been primed, but hardly expected to be shouting back, trying to keep a straight face, "Brave ... Strong ... Intelligent." This was the formula for getting into Prince Johnson's "executive mansion" on the outskirts of the Liberian capital, Monrovia. But it got me in.

"Welcome to Liberia," Prince Johnson, field marshal and acting president of war-torn Liberia, said. Taking a cold can of Budweiser from his desktop fridge, he stretched out a golden knuckled hand and with a wide, toothy grin said, "Here, come

and have a beer."

This was my bizarre introduction to one of the latest of Africa's bloody civil wars. Prince Johnson was the leader of the INPFL (Independent National Patriotic Front of Liberia), or, as he jokingly put it, "I Need Prince For Liberia." At his elbow played a video of him crooning out the tune, "By the Rivers of Babylon," his features beaming. The mansion seemed like a mad combination of a Mercedes dealership (vehicles "acquired" from the late president) and a freak show, with guerrilla fighters in wigs, bouncing-bimbo presidential bodyguards, UZI-toting 10-year-olds and chained baboons about.

Prince Johnson's "rap" revolution resembled a Hollywood B-type horror film written by a scriptwriter on acid. Only this movie was too frighteningly real.

Liberia was established by American philanthropists in the last century as a black republic for freed slaves, pledged to liberty and progress. Instead, it quickly degenerated into a nationwide plantation, ruled over by the former slaves who became Americo-Liberian landowners. It was not until Master Sergeant Samuel Doe overthrew the Americo-Liberian ruling families in 1980, resulting in their beach-side executions, that indigenous Liberians ruled for the first time. But Doe's rule was even worse, dragging Liberia back to the heart of Africa's darkness. Tribal killings became commonplace.

Having rid the country of the former president and part-time cannibal, Samuel Doe, Prince became the ruler of Monrovia by grace of the West African peace keeping force, ECOMOG. Already, however, he has found himself fighting against his erstwhile comrade Charles Taylor in a bitter struggle for power.

Prince Paints the Town Red

Prince's patrol of the Monrovian suburbs is now a nightly ritual, regularly ending in death. It is a chance for him to get away from his mansion and the war by seeking adulation from the masses — along with the satisfying possibility of blowing someone away.

I was invited to accompany the presidential entourage as it set out in a cavalcade of jeeps and pick-ups, bristling with machine guns and automatic rifles. A case of Bud was loaded onto Prince's wagon. We barely got beyond the gates, when he jumped out and swapped vehicles with his heavy bevy of Liberian beauties — his personal bodyguards, who travel in the jeep behind. Why? His tape deck had jammed.

Another stop, and the field marshal relieved himself before inspecting men at one of his checkpoints. A car decked in the camouflage used by Charles Taylor — his rival — was there with the driver's door open, engine running. "Where de driver?" he asked ... (Silence) ... "Who let him go?"

Tension was in the air, and we all felt

On The Occasion of Your Induction Into Office.

God Bless The Work Of Your Hands And Save Liberia

LONG LIVE LIBERIA

Again and L
ully
BY J. N. ELLIOTT

displaced right here in our country. There are others seeking refuge in neighbouring countries, whose plight is just as collectively appalling, all due to the senseless war the Honourable Taylor waged to remove the tyrannical regime of Samuel Doe from power. Yet he claims that he is not to be held liable for share of wrongdoing.

The Honourable should know that this is the experimental stage of national leadership, and that after the prescribed 12 months, if he wants to be that rooster to crow in terms of leading this, our patronomy, then he should now roll up his sleeves and rally around

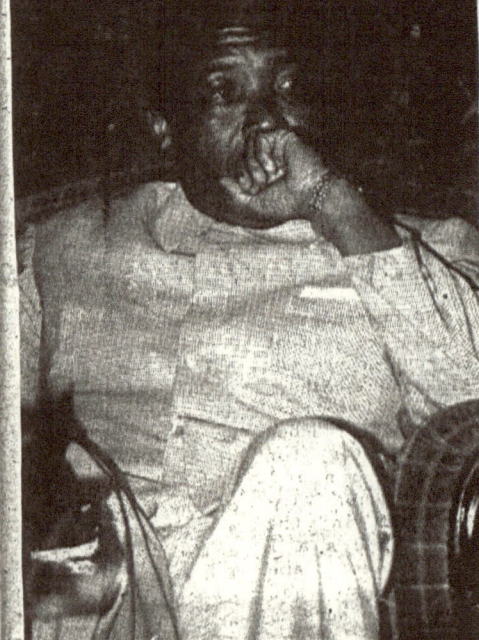

CHARLES TAYLOR VICE CHAIRMAN

whatever may have happened during the period under review.

the people to rebuild this country.

PRECIOUS COMMODITY: A Liberian girl carries water in Monrovia yesterday as water shortage continues. AP photo

Liberian army troops retreat as rebels move in

MONROVIA, Liberia — Rebels battled retreating government troops two miles from the capital yesterday, according to refugees fleeing the fighting.

Refugees from a village near Sheiffelin, a major army base 12 miles east of Monrovia, said they heard sounds of heavy artillery and submachine gunfire before soldiers ordered them to evacuate.

Rebels were advancing from Robertsfield International Airport, which they seized over the weekend after destroying the terminal with shell and mortar fire.

Yesterday's battle took place three miles from a U.S. radio transmission station used to relay diplomatic messages for sub-Saharan Africa.

Also near the rebel lines is the Omega navigational station, a major U.S. navigation facility.

The rebels so far have kept a promise not to damage U.S. government installations. A Voice of America relay station for Africa that fell behind rebel lines last week has not been threatened by the guerrillas.

New York Times 2-26, 1991

51,000 Refugees to Get Year's Reprieve in U.S.

WASHINGTON, Feb. 25 — About 51,000 people who fled political upheavals in Kuwait, Liberia and Lebanon will be permitted to remain in the United States for at least another year, Attorney General Dick Thornburgh has announced.

"This will insure that persons from those countries will not be forced to return to their homelands while present dangers exist," Mr. Thornburgh said in his announcement on Friday.

He granted the refugees temporary residency status for a period of one year based on his authority under the Immigration Act of 1990. The law, enacted last November, permits the Attorney General to grant such residency to aliens from countries subject to armed conflict, natural disasters or other extraordinary conditions.

Citizens of the three countries will be eligible whether they entered the United States as short-term legal visitors whose visas have expired or as illegal aliens. The new protected status means that they will not be subject to deportation proceedings and will be granted work authorization permits.

There is no starting date for the program, which will take effect as soon as regulations are formally published in the Federal Register. At the end of a year, the Attorney General can extend the residency status or terminate the program at his discretion.

Immigration officials estimate that 27,200 Lebanese, 10,100 Kuwaitis and 14,100 Liberians are eligible.

INNOCENT VICTIMS: A Liberian rebel stands over the bodies of civilians killed allegedly by government soldiers

Liberia refugees: Gov't troops killed 18

PAYNESVILLE, Liberia (AP) — Liberian refugees said government troops fired on civilians yesterday, killing 18. The troops, meanwhile, mounted a successful counterattack on rebel fighters, dashing the insurgents' hopes of seizing the capital before a African task force arrives to impose peace.

Troops from the government's 72nd Battalion advanced behind an armored car yesterday morning from their camp in the Paynesville suburb on the city's eastern outskirts and cut off a group of rebels trying to take Spriggs Payne airfield.

In your career, almost all of your writing will be reviewed by others, whether it is published or distributed via e-mail in the office. Learning to accept how others receive and interpret your words and, in turn, improve your work is key to creating effective communication.

Throughout this course, you are encouraged to submit your work to trusted colleagues and peers for their review using the Peer Feedback form on pp. 38-39 of Evergreen. (This form has also been provided for you in a downloadable format. You can retrieve it by or by clicking on the Supplemental Materials link in the left column under Course Home.)

The Peer Feedback form is helpful because it provides those who review your work with guidelines for providing constructive suggestions without revising your work for you. This is important: If your reviewers do your revisions for you, your work will never improve. However, gaining other people's objective suggestions concerning your content and organization is very helpful. Also, the peer criticism is helpful as you sharpen your writing skills. Remember, criticism in this circumstance is not a "bad" word; criticism just means evaluation and analysis.

Recommendation: Make use of the Peer Feedback sheet with each of your major writing assignments.

Journal Writing

The prewriting chapter in *Evergreen* includes a brief discussion of journal writing, an excellent method to help you move past the fear of putting your ideas on paper. While keeping a journal is not a course requirement, you are encouraged to begin one and maintain it at least through this course. You will undoubtedly find it extremely helpful in many unexpected ways.

Reviewing the Basics

Finally, every lesson in this course contains a review of basic grammar and mechanics. You are probably already familiar with the concepts in this section. Review them and practice as needed to develop your skills. You will find a brief graded section on each assignment that covers the basics in each lesson. This lesson reviews basic sentence structure. All of the other reviews will build upon this one, so be sure to look it over carefully.

Unit 1: Lesson 1—Reading Assignments

Evergreen, Chapters 1-4 and 24

Evergreen: A Guide to Writing with Readings
Author-Susan Fawcett; The writing process
Chapters 1-4 and 24; unit 1 Lesson-Reading Assignment
Manuscript-pages 19-21
Publisher:Houghton Mifflin Company
New York
Copyright: 1983, 1994, 1999 and 2002

The Writing Process

As your textbook discusses, the writing process includes the basic
steps of prewriting, writing, revising, and proofreading. These
don't always occur in a nice, neat order every time for every writer;
however, in trying to describe how writers write, these steps are
almost always present. Knowing these steps and attempting to
incorporate them into your writing will definitely improve your
writing. The main thing to remember is that you should start with
some ideas and a sense of organization; then write without worrying
about mechanics and grammar. Try to follow the notes you made
before writing, but if you sense a better organization or have a new
idea, go ahead and revise as you write. Next, read what you have
written and look critically at it; decide what works and what doesn't.
Strike out, re-order, make notes on what is missing; then write some
more. Do this until you are pleased with what you have said and
until your message makes sense to someone else. Finally, when all
of that is finished, proofread your work, make changes, and spell
check your final product.

Going Back to the Paragraph Basics

You may feel at this point in your life that being asked to focus on and write paragraphs is a little elementary; however, paragraphs are the building blocks of longer pieces of writing. If you review paragraph writing and practice it until you can do it well, you will find that organizing and developing longer pieces of writing is much easier for you.

Sometimes people think that writing is too subjective to be evaluated or that it is a creative art (and sometimes it is); however, most writing is the basic communication of needed information from one person to others. It can definitely be evaluated for good organization, specific vocabulary, standard grammar, and—most importantly—whether or not the message has been clearly communicated to the reader. And here is something to think about: Whether or not your writing is evaluated by an instructor for a grade, your writing is always being evaluated by your colleagues and supervisors in the workplace. So use this time to review and practice the basics of paragraph writing; what you learn and improve upon may surprise you!

Obtaining Peer Review/Criticism

You will be asked to write several compositions in this course, from paragraphs to essays. While developing an individual style and independent writing ability is critical, it is equally important to learn to appreciate others' review and constructive criticism of your work. ways organizd ourselves in groups for common protection and defense against enemies.

We organized and set up our own little government on common grounds in the absence of firearms. We always honored and respected leaders. Chaos was never found in our nation, as common as it is today. Life was very good.

THE REGIME OF SAMUEL KAYAN DOE FROM 1980-1990.

Though not educated in politics and administration, when the Master Seagent Doe and eleven enlisted men seized power from late president Mr. William Richard Tolbert Jr. in a "bloody Coup" in 1980, there were still a lot to be done for the Republic. It can be recorded that too many educators and educationists as well as politicians jointly misled Mr. Doe in too many things. Not to mention, his so-called "Free Education policy, and Free Tax Policy". Most in particular, the unthoughtful raising of salaries of all employees from court-messengers to university professor. The biggest and serious question was, where will the money come from to pay the salaries raised for the people when there is no tax to pay?

Having realized their own errors, the educators, educationists and politicians began to escape from the government and the country. However, Doe was left alone with no other alternative but to bring back the members of the same government whom he overthrew. In spite of all this, Doe's Administration was first to give Liberia its own "currency." This helped whole lots to speed up development programs in the Republic. For one reason the currency couldn't be used outside Liberia. The next very important development made by the Doe's administration was the introduction of the "Multiparty System." This nation has never had a free multiparty system in practice for one hundred thrity and three years since it became an independence nation.

Thanks be to the Doe's administration for this political development, though he was not a politician but soldier. The leadership intention of late president Samuel Kanyan Doe was very pleasant.But those whom he worked with had different intentions; this made it very difficult for his administration. The best he realized this too late. They always reminded him of his errors and enemies in government. If Doe was left alone without too many advicors, he would have done his best. Too many advisors misled Mr. Doe unto death, even the death of the gun. As Napoleon Bonaparte said, "I am a child of destiny, I only make mistakes when I listen to several advisors." It is clear that the betrayer of the Great Lord and Master Jesus Christ did not come from without but within. So was president Samuel K.Doe. His murderer did not come from his political opponents, but from within his administration.

It is true that Mr. Doe will be remembered for two specific things if not all his works. I strongly suggest that he be remembered for his ideas and creation of "Currency and multiparty system." Though he was shapely criticized by his political opponents as you will read or may have read in this book. I do believe that he did his best and must be given credit.

MR. CHARLES G. TAYLOR
AND THE REBEL FORCES
1989-1996.

There is a saying, "stupid anger makes us to do stupid things and regret there after. Do not let the sun go down on your anger. Tommy Lasorda, says.' The difference between the impossible and the possible lies in a man's determination." Be like a postage stamp, stick to something until you get there. Charles Taylor acted like a postage stamp. He got stuck on the Liberian Revolution until he entered the Executive Mansion. What is the most important thing in communication? It is to hear what isn't been said. Otherwise, they will be surely deceived.

The task of a leader is to create an environment that is conducive to self-motivation. As a leader, the important thing is not what happen when you are there, but what happen when you are not there. It was in the case with Mr. Charles Taylor during the civil war/rebel invasions. Let's talk a little about the "courage." What is courage in itself? Courage is not the absence of fear; rather it is the ability to take action in the face of fear. I am tired of hearing about men with the courage of their convictions. Nero and Caligula and Attila and Hitler had the courage to examine their convictions; but not one of them had the courage to change them, which is the true test of character.

At this time in the history of Liberia, we need an "innovator, not a visionary. An innovator is an individual who has the capacity not just of envisioning the future in an abstract, day-dreaming, fantasizing kind of way, but has the interest and the capability and the drive to actually do something about that vision. Remember, innovation is not a random process. Whenever it works, it does so because somebody has identified a real need, and found a way to bring new ideas or new technologies to bear on that need.

On the other hand, innovation is resisted by individuals who are unwilling to risk the status they have achieved and jealsously guard their own job against any change. Leadership ideas are like hen. You get a hen and learn how to maintain her, and pretty soon a dozen of chickens. I'm never impressed with the power of a leadership. I am impressed with the power of ideas. Let's not forget that it doesn't necessarily take a trained expert to come up with the best ideas. Likewise, it doesn't necessarily require only a leader to come up with the best idea for the development of a nation. Everybody must work together for the benefit of the whole.

Some diplomates say Taylor consciously sparked tribal conflict by invading northeastern Nimba County, the Gio and Mano heartland and the spawning ground for an abortive coup attempt in 1985. They say Taylor knew that Doe, a poorly educated former army master sergeant who seized power in a bloody coup in 1980, would retaliate in a manner that would allienate local residents and force them into the rebel camp. The bloody attacks Doe launched in Nimba had just that effect, diplomats said.

FEW SIGNS OF HOPE AS TURMOIL
AND FAMINE STALK AFRICA

From North to south, east to west, Africa is wracked by seemingly unending turmoil and political unrest. In many countries, drought and poverty worsen the agony—and relief supplies fall casualty to civil war. A few signs of hope shine out like beacons. In South Africa, the white government is taking steps to dismantle the apartheid system that enshrines white privilege and supremacy but black is killing black as their leaders via for political leadership.

In Chad, a conflict with Libya that has lasted 17 years may be drawing to an end—but in Ethiopia and Liberia bitter fighting rages on. Somalia's vast improverished land is mostly under rebel control, and fighting continues in southern Sudan. The newest conflict in Africa is a rebel invasion of tiny Rwanda. In the south of the continent rebel armies wage civil war in Mozambique and Angola, although diplomats say military action in both conflicts appear to have lessened since peace talks started this year—1990. At the same time, Reuter correspondents sent the following reports from old and new trouble spots.

Rwanda; this hilly central African country (populations) seven million became the continent's latest venue for war when a rebel forces invaded on October 1,1990. By the end of the month the rebel forces, composed mostly of exiled members of the country's minority Tutsi tribe who deserted the Ugandan army to launch their campaign, were firmly entrenched in a northeast of the former Belgian Colony. The rebels said they were campaigning for Rwandan citizenship and the overthrow of President Juvenal Habyarimana, who they called corrupt and undemocratic.

The government accused the rebels of tryingto re-install Tutsi leadership which prevailed before a revolt by the majority of the Hutu tribe in 1959. Diplomatic efforts to end the conflict were launched rapidly and both sides agreed in principle to a cease-fire. But the government later accused rebels of truce violation and called for an international monitoring force. Ethiopia; is the cockpit for two of Africa's most bitter conflict in—Eritrea and Tiggray. In Eritea, guerrillas have been fighting since 1962 for independence for the former Italian colony, Africa's longest-running civil war.

AN OPEN LETTER TO PRESIDENT CLINTON

An Appeal To Save Liberia

Dear Mr. President:

There are pictures of you with little Irish girls in the papers throughout your visit to Northern Ireland. The little lassies' faces seem joyous, less tense, very tranquil and fearless. They laughed and jumped for joy as they ran to greet you. In the children's eyes we see an absence of fear. The children are less apprehensive for they see no more danger from the groups that have senselessly destroyed their neighborhoods, putting the innocent lives of their unfortunate friends to an abrupt halt. Then there is a little girl who read a message to you. What a grand sight! The children will no longer worry about problems caused by grown-ups in their infancy, at least not until they become grown-ups themselves. For now, they will grow up in peace. The American peacemaker has come and assured them that the barbarism that has plagued Northern Ireland for decades will abate.

Further determined to curb the barbarism in Bosnia and despite opposition in Congress, you convened a meeting with the parties at war where an agreement was signed to end the four-year-old Bosnian conflict. Then you arranged for U.S. troops to watch over the peace process in Bosnia. Mr. President, your efforts to join free, democratic nations against the "forces of disintegration" is laudable. Our congratulations are in order for the magnitude of your diligence. Certainly, First Lady Mrs. Clinton will share credit, for she has been supportive.

Yet, Mr. President, other world communities, especially the Liberian community in the Americas, has watched your activities closely. We have equally watched the activities of administrations before yours, most importantly that of former President George Bush. We watched with interest in 1992 as America galvanized the international community and

(Continued on page 11)

Orphaned and helpless young Liberian refugees in the Ivory Coast

LIBERIA:
A BRIEF HISTORY

IN THE BEST OF TIMES, the interior of Liberia is a beautiful environment. It is a land full of dark-green forests, hills, mountains, rivers, and waters.

The farmers use the forest for subsistence farming. The soil of Liberia is incredibly rich for[12] varieties of farm crops. This nation is one of the African continent's richest countries in log of all kinds[13]. This piece of land is known for its natural mineral resources: the gold, diamonds, iron ore, aluminum and many others.

This region was discovered by a Portuguese slave-trader in 1664; who then named it, the "GRAIN COAST". The name Liberia derived from a Latin word. "LIBER" means "FREE". This country has been a free country from its initial founding. However, it was later[14] taken over, redefined and named by the American Colonization Society—ACS, as the home of the free slaves from the continent of North America in 1822.

Since then, this nation is known in world history as the first Negro Republic. Frankly, this nation belongs to all black people, especially the black Americans. Liberia is bounded by the Atlantic Ocean on the South; the French Republic of Guinea on the North; the French Republic of the Ivory Coast on the East; the West, Sierra Leone.

In spite of the wealth of the soil and forest, the Liberians were de-pressingly poor. But the sting of poverty was removed by the fact that they were more or less on the same level with other peoples of the area. At least everyone lived in mud homes and ate the same low or poor diet.

The datums of Liberia show the following records definitely. The population was approximately 2,874,881 in the month of July, 1993. The birth rate also was 43.9 births per 1,000 population in the same 1993. Population growth rate was also 3.37%. Death rate was 12.38 deaths per 1,000 population. With a net migration rate of 2.15 migrants per 1,000 population.

The infant mortality rate was 115.9 deaths per 1000 live births as estimated in 1993. The life expectancy at birth was a *total* of 57.28 years; male, 54.88 years; female, 59.76 years. The sum total fertility rate of 6.42 children born per woman was estimated in the year 1993.

The ethnic divisions of Liberia include the following indigenous African tribes (95% including Kpelle, Bassa, Gio, Mano, Kru, Grebo, Krahn, Gola, Gbandi, Loma, Kissi, Vai, and Bella), Americo-Liberians 5% descendants of repatriated slaves).

Religion is comprised of 70% traditional, 20% Christian and 10% Muslim. Languages spoken are English (official), Niger-Congo language group—about 20% of local languages come from this group.

The literacy age is about 15 years and over, can read and write in the year 1990. The total population who can read and write is about 40%; male 50% and female 29%. Labor force is 510,000 including 220,000 in the monetary economy by occupation; agriculture 70.5%, services 10.8%, industry and commerce 4.5%, other 14.2%.

Note : The disappointment perhaps, for the typical Liberian is non-African foreigners who hold about ninety-five per cent of the top-level management and engineering jobs, 52% of the population of working age.

THE GOVERNMENT

Unlike that of the United States of America, Liberia is governed by a "Unitary" form of government headed by a president, vice president, cabinet and other elected local chiefs. The govenment is divided into three branches; the Executive branch, headed by a president; the Legislative branch is bicameral. National Assembly consists of an upper house or Senate and a lower house or House of Representatives.

The Judicial branch, the people's Supreme Court which is also headed by a Chief Justice and five associate justices. These branches[18] interact with each other. After the overthrow of the late president Mr. William R. Tolbert Jr. on 12 April, 1980, the constitution, which has served the nation as its working tool, was illegally suspended for an indefinite time. The then PRC government headed by Master Sgt. Samuel K. Doe, unthoughtfully decided to reject this government legal document which has served this country for about one hundred and thirty-three unbroken years.

Having banned this legal document, a special committee was set-up by the Head of State, Master Sgt. Samuel K. Doe with the help of the PRC high ranking officers who seem not to have actually had better knowledge and experience in government. According to reliable sources, the constitution was to be abolished entirely. Dr. Amos Sawyer, a professor of political science at the University of Liberia at the time, was appointed by the then head of state to chair the committee.

This committee became known throughout the country as the "Draft Constitution Committee." Dr. Sawyer and his committee members slightly overlooked the importance of a civilian contesting against a military person in power controlling guns. Dr. Sawyer and his group having failed to recognize this very vital fact, Mr. Samuel K. Doe took this to his advantage. Hence, they empowered Mr. Doe to form his own Political Party and contest for the presidency under one single condition; if he (Doe) could agree to resign from the military into a so-called civilian life, while still a head of state for the country.

Mr. Doe then seized the opportunity to quickly resign in theory while emotionally and inwardly remaining a soldier. Mr. Samuel K. Doe was then told to form a Political Party of his own to run for the presidency in 1985. However, Mr. Doe did not win the election for president. He was left with no other alternative but to again use his same gun which brought him to power in 1980. With the force of the gun, Mr. Doe started to gamble that the government would sell the seats in both houses to those whom he (Doe) felt would possibly give him some money. He didn't consider the interest of the masses or voters. This became very outrageous throughout the nation. It created serious political disagreements among politicians and their supporters as well. As a result, the late Doe's regime lost both national and international creditability.

This led him to exercise absolute power as a dictator, instead of a Democrat. Thus, he tried to change the nation's form of government in practice to autocratic form. Doe and his clique started to institute the practice of Demonism. A practice which was secretly legalized by the late President Tubman's administration. Today, 52 years later, we are back into a practice which we fled and escaped once. Rebellion against government has brought us back into demonism in Liberia again. We are told by reliable sources that the rebel soldiers of Mr. Charles Taylor and his collaborators are dining upon human hearts.

Demonism has taken the place of Christianity in Liberia today. The Economic Community of West African States (ECOWAS) has again reinstated Dr. Sawyer and his committee members in the Peace process.

By ordering down Monrovia, the warring faction leaders then, left their loyal troops in the bushes with their arms. Here we see the result: the "FIGHTING IS RENEWED". This leads me or anybody to believe that we Africans, especially Liberian for that matter, do not learn from the mistakes of the past because we are always busy making new ones. This is why the African continent will never have genuine peace. It is quite disgusting—we as a nation (Liberia) have a government similar to that of the United States of America, but do not practice same. The constitution of any nation ought to be regarded by everybody as a mirror to carefully use in order to see oneself as a loyal citizen. Also to be ready to immediately rectify whatsoever errors the individual sees in his or her daily activities. Disappointedly, too many people don't seem to agree with this statement.

THE WHITE CAR TO THE DEVIL ROCK

During the administration of the late president, Mr. William V. S. Tubman, too many ritualistic killings went on in Liberia unchecked. An evil society was formed by local government officials called "The White Car to the Devil Rock." Too many innocent citizens, especially children and women, lost their lives in the county of Maryland.

This society continued its evil operations until Tubman's death in July 1972. After which, when Mr. William R. Tolbert Jr. took over the presidency in the same year and exposed the secret of the society in 1976 when he ordered some of the leading members of the society to be brought to justice for murdering a young musician. Seven of those brought to trial were found guilty of murder: execution by hanging was sentenced by the court and then approved by President Tolbert.

The seven members were publicly hanged in the city of Harper, Marvland County. This created numerous enemies in government against the president. All through his administration, Tubman knew about this society, but did nothing to eradicate its operation in the interior county of Maryland for 27 unbroken years. The poor taxpayers lives were never secure. Justice was often denied to them. This resulted in the forming of many secret societies in the land.

Thank God, the Revelator, William R. Tolbert Jr., took over the nation's presidency in 1972. He was there now to deliver the poor children and women from the evil forces. The White Car was a phrase often used by the Marylanders to indicate the presence of danger. The Devil Rock also indicated a place of danger for life. It was vividly known that anybody who was taken to this place was never going to live to tell the story. This unacceptable and unbearable behavior of the past administrations built in the minority feelings of rejection, being unwanted and resentment. Together these have resulted in political urnest and widespread civil conflict. The past administration of Tubman cannot nor should ever be exempted from this civil conflict in Liberia. It seriously contributed used to the civil war which has destroyed nearly 75% or more of the population of Liberia.

The White Car carried many innocent citizens and residents of Liberia to the "Devil Rock" likewise, the present gun has and is carrying many peaceful innocent citizens, residents and friends to the grave. Therefore, the relationship which exists between the White Car and the Liberian Civil Conflict is as close as the eye is to the nose. One can never distinguish the evil behavior of the two.

When Tubman became president in 1943, the nation was in her darkest days. He was called the national government of Liberia by the indigeneous tribes of the Republic. The president was considered by his kinsmen as the God of the state. These misrepresentations of the government by the people, enthused the president to distance himself from the rest of the Liberian people, causing him to become very arrogant and sometimes aggressive. In the eastern county—Maryland, the consistent rumors of what was commonly known as the "White car to the devil rock" spread throughout the land.

Rampant atrocities went on in the administration which would never be mentioned in any conversation at the time. It was said if anyone ever tried to mention this the person could easily get "lost". Justice was often denied everywhere in the land. Rather, the theme of the day was "intimidation". Criminals were the best regarded and protected citizens whom the administration loved dearly. Whoever committed a crime of any kind against the masses was promoted to another, higher position without any thorough investigation.

Once upon a time in Bong County, Superintendent James Y. Gbegbeyea was charged in the embezzlement of ($8,500,000.00) eight million, five hundred thousand dollars Gbegbeyea was then transferred by the president from county superintendent to Minister of Land and Mines; where he would be able to steal more money than before.

Should we say then that President Tubman himself supported crime? Technically, he did. Technically, Tubman was sometimes a part of many criminal activities in Liberia. I can plainly recall when I was just about 12 years old, I stood by my late uncle Mr. Sumo Gaaii and saw a soldier climb on his shoulders and head. Just because he (Gaaii), missed Mr. Tubman's name and voted for his (Tubman) political opponent, Mr. Barclay. Old man Gaaii was not educated, neither could he read nor write. However, Mr. Tubman's loyal supporters expected this uneducated man to distinguish Tubman from Barclay. This is a typical form of injustice against this man. As a matter of fact, it was his right to vote for whomsoever he pleased; if only the administration was democratic in its true nature. But, since it was not democratic, rather a dictatorship, he was not allowed to exercise such rights.

After which old man Sumo Gaaii filed his civil-right violation case in the County Commissioner's court: His complaints were ignored and instead he met a nightmare; receiving a fine of no less or more than ($25.00) U.S. dollars imposed on him. This, as a child attending school with no income, indicated to me that the poor people were never protected by this administration at any point.

When seeking a better redress of this case, my uncle Sumo Gaaii believing in democratic principles, though he could never read nor write, proceeded to the next higher court. To his uttermost surprise, President Tubman ordered through one of the local officials to jail this poor taxpayer for no less than six months. This was another vivid indication of injustice in the land.

Before, the citizens of Liberia residing in the interior were often less regarded by their own government whom they often pay taxes to. These poor citizens pay taxes to a government which gives them no protection. They were denied the benefits of their taxes paid, such as good, pure drinking water, electricity, etc. Yet, they were flogged always to induce payment of taxes. I pronounce this injustice on the part of a national government in the country.

THE ORIGIN OF AFRICAN SLAVE TRADE

BEFORE the European Traders reached Africa, there was already a form of slave-trade in existence. In this chapter, we will briefly describe how this inhumane activity started. Slave-trade started in the African villages. It started with criminals. There are specifically, two classes of people who were sold into slavery. Firstly, the children of a man's sister, who are universally known as nephew and niece. And secondly, criminals.

Slavery was the penalty for committing a crime which was duly pronounced by the villagers as being serious or a felony in both first and second degrees, such as murdering of another person or persons willfully, raping of children or women habitually, destroying of live trees or crops, killing of domestic animals against the sure concern and consent of their rightful owners, consistent invading of another person's land (territory)—trespassing, stealing, covetness, etc.

The above mentioned cases and many others were decided by the respective elders to determine the guilt of the accused. If the defendant was found guilty, he was sold to a chief in another distant village, not his own. It was very rare in this case for any good and loyal citizen to be sold; rather, criminals or violent people.

Women were sold under one condition; that is when they became prostitutes. The reason was that women were very afraid of criminal activities other than prostitution. Besides prostitution, a woman would only poison her husband or lover's food whenever she felt that she was cheated. However, this charge was very difficult for the elders to prove.

The first group of people to be sold at the time was quite disgusting in that an innocent person or kid was going to suffer as a criminal when he or she had never committed a crime of any kind. Why sell your sister's child for little or nothing when you should be protecting them? Whenever the African man got out of money, he often turned to his sister's children for economic reasons.

The girls were legally married to men not of their choice by the uncle. Most often the nephew was sold for rice, cassava and other things his uncle needed. This wicked behavior continued for centuries.

Finally, the white people came to Africa to trade for gold, diamonds and other minerals. The white men asked the tribesmen to provide them a labor force to carry their materials. Then the tribesmen requested payment in return, offering their slaves to the white men for little or nothing. When the Europeans saw that this was a good and cheap business and more profitable for them, they entered into it with the African chiefs. Now slave-trade had started between the Europeans and the African kinsmen.

You would see a string of African slaves coming down to the coast on ropes to be sold to the European traders. The men's families were crying and screaming for their release or freedom. But, unfortunately for the men and their loved ones, the wicked tribal chiefs paid no mind. Rather, the chiefs continue to say take them away forever. The morning of their departure was the greatest nightmare for their children, wives and other relatives.

It was wicked and inhumane behavior on the part of these leaders. The most disgusting and frustrating days in the lives of slaves were the days of departure from among their own people and from their land of nativity because they had no hope of reunion. They are forever gone. Realizing that they will never see them again, their loved ones bid them farewell, we love you, we will remember you in our prayers and sacrifices. The ghost of our people who passed away be with you forever.

The wicked chiefs continued to say, let me hear my ears; let them go immediately and forever. Away with them forever. The noises of crying and screaming, hitting the ground in tears, people rolling on the ground in the grass and running back into the green forest seeking comfort. The African Kings often used their kinsmen as properties; not taxpayers and loyal citizens.

Will a better life ever exist on this continent? Today, African boys, men, girls and women are selfishly acquiring education to hold their brothers and sisters, and perhaps, parents hostage and enslave them. It is a pity that as life continues to gradually change for the best, African leaders in the family, the educational institutions, associations, organizations, even the churches, and most importantly, their national governments are still intending to live cruel, mean and barbarian lives

Back to hell. Liberia as a Christian nation, has gone back again into hell fire. Since April 12, 1980, Liberia has returned to hell on earth instead of going forward to heaven. Since then, the nation is still sinking deep down into hell each and every day. On April 13, 1980, you would see noble men tied on light poles at the coconut plantations outside Monrovia, near the Atlantic Ocean, waiting for their executions. Their wives, children, friends and other relatives are crying, sharing tears; while gunmen are chasing them away from the scene.

Soldiers were chasing people in the city of Monrovia and everywhere in Liberia. Scholarships were taken away from students in high school, colleges and universities, at which time I had just enrolled at the Cuttington University College in the nursing department. Having graduated from Konola Academy Mission of Seventh Day Adventists 1972, as a "B" plus student, I also received a personal scholarship from Mr. William R. Tolbert Jr. that placed me on the list of victims of the coup. We were seen individually escaping for our lives.

As I was working in the Phebe Hospital in 1980, I witnessed the cruel execution of a man who was shot in the legs and brought to the hospital for medical attention. He was hunted by enemy soldiers.

Again, a guaranteed Peace is promised. Approximately 60 to 70 Peace accords have failed the Liberian people. Promises which should have led to a genuine peace. Each peace accord was always said to be guaranteed. Would Liberians ever trust or believe any peace accord promise again? I seriously doubt this. Having keenly and closely followed this civil-war[106] from its start to present, I would seriously doubt if there will ever be any guaranteed peace due to the existence of numerous warlord factions. One thing I have observed that they are striving toward is power.

THE EDUCATION SYSTEM
FROM 1980

IF THIS PHILOSOPHY of education is considered to be true, "education is the key to knowledge," then Liberia's future is threatened. Education or educators are murdered each and every day since April 12, 1980. Those educationists and educators who have gone to the grave beyond have out numbered the living ones. Beginning December 24, 1989, educational materials and buildings have been senselessly destroyed every day in the nation. A library was once burned to ashes on the very campus of the University of Liberia publicly in 1990, demoralizing all instructional materials thereafter.

School buildings were bombed throughout the nation. The Cuttington University College women and men dormitories were burned down into ashes in October, 1994, unthoughtfully. I saw rebel soldiers whom people are obliged to defend and protect with lies, put books, school desks, chairs, maps and globes on fire senselessly in the city of Gbarnga.

Using graduation gowns as their daily patrol uniforms, they go from one village to another robbing the poor villagers. It can be recorded that during the April 12, 1980 coup, Liberia lost her international creditability in education in the international community. Noble men were tied on light poles and shot to death in the city of Monrovia for what was called "rampant corruption and misuse of public office". After which the worse corruption of tribalism, nepotism, misuse of public funds, properties, intimidation with the use of fire arms, and ritualistic killings arose throughout the Republic.

The unacceptable practices of carnivorousness and harassment widely spread in most high places in the nation. Ritualistic killings which were seriously opposed by the past government were refrained everywhere in Liberia. The national standard of education dropped from 80% down to 50% in less than five years of the PRC government tenure. During the political-military era of Liberia, education became less regarded and abused. The wrongful use of fire arms were the only standard of education.

Educational corruption was the common song of the day beginning with the Executive Mansion down to the town chief's court. It was announced by the great University of Liberia radio December, 1989, that late president Samuel Kanyan Doe had completed his discipline for a bachelor of art degree in political science in Liberia. It was amazing when the board of trustees of the University of Liberia announced that Doe came first in the graduating class—a man who never sat in the classroom for a single lecture for more than a month.

This became very outrageous among the graduates; it also became habitual for many Liberians at home and abroad to always buy or crook a degree. It is a shame, and perhaps educational crime, for anyone to possess a document of any kind which he or she cannot defend practically.

Free education was pronounced by the then head of state, Master/Sgt. Samuel Kanyan Doe in 1980 immediately after the April 12 coup d'etat. The question that came to the minds of many educated, experienced Liberians and friends of Liberia was, had the government given careful study to this subject. Of course not. According to some political analysts, this was done with the intention of gaining high momen-tum in the community. On the other hand, some educated Liberians have planned to mislead the semi-educated head of state and the Liberian public.

The economists, the financial specialists and the politicians were probably responsible for this act if they were consulted and listened to by the administration. While it is true that many African leaders turn deaf ears to their consultants and ordinary citizens, it is also true that African leaders are known to be dictative, arrogant, aggressive and tyrannical.

The late president Mr. Samuel Kanyan Doe of Liberia happened to be one of those. I am told sincerely that once upon a time, he offered a nice slap in one senator's ear for attempting to advise him on certain political issues. I will, therefore, want to think that due to the fear of his rusty hand, they refused to advise him (Doe) from this day onward. As a matter of fact, no man will ever appreciate the rusty fingers of another man on his body. Even though I am not speaking on their behalf, up to now I still wonder how a national government could possibly operate successfully without taxes. Mr. Doe deleted taxes in his administration and then raised the salaries of employees.

I cannot still understand the possibility of a national government operating genuinely without taxes being paid by its citizens. This was the most unreasonable, thoughtless, and maybe deceitful act any government could ever carry out in any country. The result of this great error was economic disaster upon the nation of Liberia. This country has yet to recover from this disease of the late Doe's crazy administration.

Can a national government operate on false hope and survive? No, national government can never survive on false hope. The taxpayers' patience will sooner or later run out after a few years. It is a sad thing that the operating policy of the past administration in Liberia has always been based on false hope and lies. I suppose this would be some of the contributing factors which led to the civil war in 1989.

Disappointingly for the poor Liberian people, here come again another universal brutal group of liars. They claim to be peace or freedom fighters; they went on a rampage to murder poor people for their own foodstuffs. They claim to be their redeemers but, inwardly, they are nothing but a group of murderers. I am very sorry for the future of this nation of Liberia. I suppose the one who brought the idea did not really intend it to be this way.

I am afraid to say that he is disappointed in these figures. As one speaker put it this way, "It is easy to train a man to do evil, but it is very hard to train a man to love because men are accustomed to doing evil." Mr. Taylor might never have intended preparing terrorists for the future of Liberia, but it has just become a nightmare for him.

As one old man said to me on one occasion, "These Mano and Gio people have long been trying to cause more danger in this country, but Taylor did not know at first, they are going to kill all the people before they stop."

In our world today, I cannot see the possibility of any government depending only on arms and corruption to rule a country like Liberia and then succeed in doing such. I am told by very reliable individuals that the rebel soldiers of the NPFL are now eating human heart just as the late Samuel Kanyan Doe and his royal troops did. The youths of Liberia are only educated in using fire arms nowadays instead of learning how to use pencil and copybook. Can we build a nation today with only armed men and women who do not know how to read or write?

If these children who are of school age cannot think of school nowadays instead of who they can kill and eat some parts, then where are we going now my fellow Liberians? A nation in which the principles of Christianity were practiced and observed everywhere, I cannot see the sure possibility of someone changing these children from evil practices to becoming good and loyal citizens of Liberia.

One can see the great disappointment in the future of this nation. In this regard, each and every thoughtful and peace-loving Liberian has a grave responsibility to undertake preparing the future generation of his nation. As you may see vividly, they have been miseducated by evil forces for their personal gains. The motives of these people are very evil and dangerous for any nation in our world today. It is a great shame that Liberia as a Christian nation has become a den of demons, while other countries that were considered by the world as being heathen are getting converted.

Demonism has become the most common practice in Liberia today, since April 12, 1980. Where are the Christian churches, my people? What role are they playing in the entire episode? What message are they preaching to the citizens and the future generations of Liberia? The Christians must get up and work with a Christian zeal, fast and pray for this dying nation.

According to history, too many nations have gone astray beyond this point, and God did consider them; later they became better. There is nothing impossible for God. Germany could be a very good example for this, during World War II, when Adolf Hitler misled the people of Germany to kill all the Jews. After which the economic conditions of Germany entered into its first infliction which was a very serious predicament for the nation. However, when the Germans realized that they had been misled by Mr. Hitler, they backed out. So shall it be with the Liberians, sooner or later.

According to the Wednesday, October 19, 1994 newspaper, who was in full control of the central city of Gbarnga was unknown. Gbarnga is the capital city of Bong County, located in the center of Liberia. At this time, Gbarnga became the focus of attention for both local and foreign journalists as well as the citizens and the international community. There were claims and counter-claims by the various factions as regards to the control of the NPFL headquarters—Gbarnga.

However, the war reporter Mr. Sidiki Trawally and the ace photographer, Mr. James Momoh, took a one week tour in upper Lofa County. They finally landed in the trouble-zone, Gbarnga. After spending almost a week in the capital city of Lofa County, Voinjama, here are their reports: "In Voinjama city, Lofa County, we took off under the escort of Battalion Commander Col. Sekou Konneh. The chairman Alhaji G. V. Kromah gave instructions to his field commander, Major-General Mohammed Doumouyah to take us to Gbarnga. Prior to our departure, we saw some NPFL heavy artillery including BZT, a barrel and chaser missiles captured by ULIMO men. Carlton Karpeh, a frontline fighter, told us at his headquarters in Voinjama city that they are Taylor's supplies".

Several light weapons like AK-47 G-3s, among others, as well as trucks belonging to CRC that were also captured from them by the NPFL fighters during the fight in the city of Gbarnga. There were several displaced refugees who were in Gbarnga. They had been evacuated by the ULIMO fighters into their territory, Voinjama and other towns around Gbarnga; including Belefanai, Gbalatuah and Wensue. It can be recorded that most of these atrocities happened at around October 6, 1994. It also indicates that on Thursday, October 6, 1994, at the precise hour of 10:45 p.m., a Nissan patrol Jeep, once owned by an official of NPFL carrying Ivorian plates was also found in ULIMO territory. There was indication that it was used by the medias upon their arrival, even though it was not in good condition. Which forced them to spend the night at Bruzeewein, a little village on the Voinjama, Zorzor highway.

The following day which was Friday, some residents of the area assisted the team with grass to substitute for air for the tire, because there was no air available. Again, there was another shortage of air in Luyamah. The exercise was repeated. Even in another village, Konia, the same problem was repeated and its usual method was followed. This was going on already in the city of Zorzor at 5:52 a.m., where the night was spent. The journey continues on Saturday and by 9:00 a.m. a Land Rover Jeep was provided for the trip to Gbarnga. On the way to Gbarnga, several stops were made; first, at Salayea, a village inhabited by both the Kpelle and Loma ethnic groups. Atrocities have also occurred in this area just as elsewhere along the highway from Voinjama.

Leaving structures covered with grass, only ULIMO fighters are seen in this area, with no civilians around. The civilians are said to have fled when the Lofa Defense Force (LDF) attacked the area Sukromu town, a village before Salayea town on the Zorzor Voinjama highway which is no more. In another town called Gorlue, a similar environment as in Salayea exists, but few structures are still in shape. No civilians can be found in Gangro town, a little village close to the St. Paul River which divides Lofa and Bong Counties.

From this point onward, we are now entering into the actual home of great atrocities—Bong County.

(ECOMOG) was under attack, and they were sending out warnings to all the warring factions, NPFL, ULIMO, and others to keep out of the renewed fighting. It was also reported by the paper that three ECOMOG soldiers have been killed in the renewed fighting.

The paper further indicates that the rebel soldiers of Charles Taylor and A.G.V. Kroma and others have no intention of accepting the idea of disarmament. The paper also explained that a certain 17-year-old rebel soldier, when interviewed by the paper, clearly stated, "I cannot and will not lay down my gun." When asked by a foreign journalist why the mean fighter exclaimed, "Because I use this gun to get whatever my family and I need."

In this connection, the fighters from both sides are now considering their arms as the only means through which they can make a living. The 17-year-old fighter maintains that if he has to kill in order for he and his family to survive, he will forever continue to do so until his last day. Who knows the last day of this little demon; nobody. I seriously believe that this little monster has also passed his demonistic ideas to his fellow fighters, too.

This shows that Liberia is in danger for the rest of the century. The warring factions have put Liberia on the death road. The past administration of President William V. S. Tubman and the regime of the late Head of State Samuel Kanyan Doe, who later proclaimed himself president in 1985, built the road to hell for the nation. The late President William Richard Tolbert, Jr., the one-time Vice President and successor of Tubman, became the only "Revelator" in Liberia during his administration. He promoted democracy.

President Tolbert's three years as president were equivalent to Tubman's 28 years as president. Tolbert revealed to the nation every secret and dirty deed that he met in the Executive Mansion. This act created more and more enemies for him in high places in government. When life failed his perpetrators and adversaries in the United States of America, they turned to him and accused him of making life hard for the people of Liberia. The perpetrators pretended that they were for the Liberian people.

President Tolbert encouraged all Liberians to be self-sufficient in food production. "A government that cannot feed its citizens is not a government." He saw the bright future of the nation which his predecessors did not see. The assassination of Tolbert was the heaviest blow to hit the Liberian society since 1822. Accordingly, a letter was addressed to the Interim Government by a group called "United Voice of Liberia." It reads:

Dear Mr. Chairman,

We wish to congratulate you for the good works you are involved with for our country and its people. In spite of all, we stand with you in anything you would wish that we Liberians in the United States do to help your administration end the crisis. However, we will highly appreciate it if you were to permit us to freely express our common ideas and feelings in this respectful manner. Sir, in as much as we respect and honor your office, we would like to inform you that we owe no respect to any organization, group or government which has no regard for democratic principles, especially human rights and peace. We have seen, read or heard enough of atrocities rampantly committed and still on going in Liberia. We wish that this would be the time for your administration to take drastic measures against same.

The Interim Government ought to take a stand against these unbearable, inhumane and demonistic attitudes.

Too many errors were made during the so-called peace conferences held in Bamako, Mali, Yamousokro, Ivory Coast, Benin, Togoland, (Cotonou) Akosombo, Ghana, and above all, in Monrovia. We have observed that at no time were human rights violations ever mentioned on any of the numerous peace agendas, nor in discussions.

Worst of all was when the Peacekeeping Monitors (ECOMOG) started to train and prepare dissidents inside Liberia, arming them as well. This act on the part of ECOMOG shocks everybody; it also clearly indicates that ECOMOG's mission was not to monitor Peace, rather to create chaos. It can be recorded that this institution of "peace" went on a rampage, bombing civilians throughout the nation. This is a clear indication of human rights violations.

We must accept the fact in spite of all these acts in the nation that there can be no hope of winning a single victory of genuine peace and freedom without truly addressing and overcoming a desperate resistance on the part of the warlords. And that victory and peace will not come of itself but only as a result of a bitter struggle on behalf of the oppressed people in the overcoming of tribal and military discrimination.

Honestly, the Interim Government is liable to question the matter if drastic measures are not taken to address some of these issues. Many Liberians believe that the NPFL leadership was the only obstacle to peace in Liberia; but it is now clear that their views on the situation were not truth. We continue to receive a very strong signal from the NPFL leadership that they are willing to cooperate with the Interim Government, which leadership is now wholly and surely involved with the peace process in Monrovia.

However, we wish you the best of success in your administration that you may deliver our poor people from the intimidation of the gunmen.

Good luck

"United Voice of Liberia"
Baltimore, MD, U.S.A.

CONCLUSIONS

THE SOLUTION OF LIBERIA'S PROBLEMS was never the execution of the thirteen noble men on April 14, 1980. Neither was it the assassination of President William Richard Tolbert, Jr. on April 12, 1980. The coming to power of the so-called PRC regime of Mr. Samuel Kanyan Doe was one of the worst nightmares Liberians have ever experienced.

While the December 24, 1989, invasion by the NPFL was not the solution, rather it was another nightmare. Furthermore, the number of atrocities have increased. From this point onward, Liberians must learn to find a solution to their political problems, rather than another coup d'etat or civil war.

Coup d'etat and civil crisis will never settle the political problems nor the administrative ones in Africa. All lead to a disastrous chaos which always results in massacre.

The massive destruction of properties which hit the nation in 1980 and 1989 to the present is a clear indication that we can never solve our political problems through this medium. Rather it has created a long setback of community development and progress.

The assassinations of leaders have never helped the Africa of yester-year; neither will it help the Africa of today. Let's be civilized, modernized and spiritual in all our dealings as Christians. Vandalism, heathenism, demonism and barbaric attitudes should never again be supported by Liberians as now. Nobody again, forever, may seek the leadership of Liberia through the use of arms. Liberia is not a heathen nation; it is a sure long-term Christian nation.

The founding fathers of this nation of Liberia did not intend to build a den of demons. Liberia, being the first Negro Republic in Africa, should be able to set a good example for other nations. This nation has been and is still known as the first Negro Republic in the whole of Africa since July 26, 1847; through the endless blessings and mercy of God.

Long live the Republic of Liberia, Africa; may God bless and keep safe the nation while maintaining the continent of Africa in peace. May the souls of those who have gone to the grave beyond rest in peace in the bosom of our father Abraham. May our hopes be strong and faithful forever.

AUTOBIOGRAPHICAL NOTE
1995

I WAS BORN IN KAYATA, Kpoyorquelly Clan, Bong County, Liberia, on 28 November 1948. My father, Togba Geelesey, was a farmer and a monogamist with a single wife. Neither he nor my mother ever went to school. My father left in 1951 on the account of a free labor as it was the usual habit of the local government officials in the rural areas.

After which Lablah Gamesia, then a very strong leading man of the village, became my guardian and step-father. Flomo Jackson, the Sectional or Chiefdom Clerk of Zota District at the time, and cousin of my mother, is, according to Kpelle custom, my uncle.

I am a sophomore student at Morgan State University in the Telecommunications Department. I also did four semesters of studies at Cuttington University College in Liberia, from 1980 to 81. I did two years training at the Lutheran Hospital School of Practical Nursing and graduated January 21, 1980. Before then, I studied medical laboratory science at the same hospital—Phebe from 1976 to 77, and graduated as a lab assistant.

Immediately following my high school studies and graduation in 1972, I enrolled at the Seventh Day Adventist Seminar in Monrovia in 1973 specifically studying "Systematic Theology" and obtained a Special Certificate December, 1974. I married Cecelia, daughter of John Natie Dro of Grand Bassa County, Liberia. I have four children, three by a former marriage and one with Cecelia.

My political and editorial interests were first aroused when I listened to my grandfather (Juahquellie Kpalaine) and other elders of our tribe (Kpelle) in my village as a child. They often talked of tribal war and the good old days before the arrival of the settlers. Though there were tribal conflicts at times, our people lived peacefully under the democratic leadership of the kings and councilmen and moved freely all through the land.

The country was always theirs; not for gunmen. We enjoyed the palm wine, forests, rivers and the land, days and nights. We set Koo (group of farmers working together) without any fear of guns. We al- a civilian review commission to purge the military of human rights abusers. Although the circumstances in Liberia differ, important lessons can be learned from the role human rights played in El Salvador's peace process, especially the effort to seek accountability.

The cycles of abuse in Liberia have been reported so many times but those responsible continue to act with impunity. Killers continue to kill, because there is no accountability, and never has been. Meanwhile, the international community becomes complicit in the violence.

RECOMMENDATIONS TO ECOMOG

ECOMOG should launch an immediate investigation into the air attacks on civilians and civilian targets, as well as violations of medical neutrality, by its forces in NPFL territory and make its findings public.

Accountability for past human rights abuses by all sides to the conflict must be pursued, and the establishment of some form of Truth Commission should be considered.

Human rights guarantees must be incorporated into the peace process.

A full investigation should be conducted into the killing of Brian Gamham.

All warring factions—the NPFL and ULIMO—must be disarmed and demobilized in a systematic and even-handed manner. ECOMOG must cease supplying arms or ammunition to any of the warring parties.

Humanitarian assistance must be permitted to reach civilians throughout Liberia, including the population of displaced persons in NPFL territory. In addition, ECOMOG must ensure the security of relief operations to the best of its ability, and must never subject them to attack by ECOMOG planes.

ECOMOG should assist in the repatriation of refugees from neighboring countries and the return of internally displaced persons.

The mandate of the proposed U.N. cease-fire monitors should be expanded to include human rights monitoring and documentation. The international community—especially the United States and the United Nations Security Council—must bring pressure to bear on both the ECOMOG commanders and the ECOWAS heads of state to use their leverage to stop the ULIMO and AFL advance and to ensure that ECOMOG reaches Nimba County first and acts in accordance with international humanitarian law.

RECOMMENDATIONS TO THE UNITED STATES

The United States must use its leverage with the ECOWAS countries, especially given the Administration's request for $12 million in aid for ECOWAS's peacekeeping activities, to pressure ECOMOG on Human Rights Action.

The United States should apply its approach for the Vienna Conference on Human Rights, described in the draft U.S. Human Rights Action Plan, which call for human rights to be "an integrated element of all U.N. peacekeeping, humanitarian, conflict resolution, elections monitoring, development programs, and other activities."

DEMOCRATISING LIBERIA

In the letter "Democracy in Africa" (West Africa, December 18) the author rightly spotted the omission of Liberia in Prof. David West's "Prospects for Democracy in Africa." My comments will be twofold: Mr. Krua's romantic affair with democracy in pre-1980 Liberia and Prof. David West's view of ethnicity as Africa's most intractable problem.

Let me start with my country's former leadership. One of the most important objectives of the authoritarian Liberian state has always been to instill in its citizens the high degree of fear for a required level of docility. The timid population is then manipulated and exploited with little or no resistance. The wealth exploitation goes to nurture the clientelist relations of the nation. Nobody can go any further from the truth than to construe this exploitation (passivity) of the people to suggest democracy.

The autocratic regimes in Liberia, especially those of Presidents Barclay and Tubman, were particularly good at such a paternalistic mode of governance. Tolbert tried to change the political system but the establishment was not quite prepared to follow his pace. The wide support for the late Sgt. Doe on April 12, 1980 was a glaring indication of the Liberian people's desire for change. The fact that Doe did not live up to the ideals of the masses should not be seen as justifying the mis-overnance of his predecessors. True, African intellectuals have their own stake in the oppression of the African people and Liberian intellectuals are no exception. However, we do not help the situation by looking at issues through the tinted glass of blind nationalism. If we must write, as rightly suggested, then we must abide by the fundamental principle of scholarship-objectivity.

Prof. David West's paper is yet another argument for Africa's dependency. When will we begin to call the cat by its name? Africa (pre—or post-colonial) by its very nature is multi-ethnic. Our ethnic identity is only one of the multiple identities we bear as Africans. We tend to cling furiously, rather blindly, to some of these identities for two major reasons: when there is something to be gained (i.e. undue privilege) or when we feel insecure within our own societies and need solidarity to resist. African governments, in their attempts to override the popular will and perpetuate their despotic rule, have tended to play with the latent yet explosive ethnic phenomenon. The worst ethnic conflicts in Africa are not necessarily in those countries with the most ethnic-based politics. Rwanda, Burundi Somalia and Liberia, to some extent, are good recent examples.

I am personally confinced that democracy is the most human and appropriate type of political system in our world today; yet I do not claim to have arrived at this conviction by academic exploits, but by a definitely extra-academic personal decision. As a Ghanaian, I aspire for true democracy in my own 'backyard' yet it doesn't mean I consider it the only legitimate form of rule that exists in the world. Rotational presidenty is not a good or positive form of rule among forms of governance.

BURKINA FASO

The ECOMOG soldiers are related to a Chinese giant whom I watched sometime ago in a movie saying to his friend, "We are going around killing people for money but, because you are my friend, I will kill you for nothing." How would you like this friendship in your life?

The ECOMOG soldiers should be called BCADP instead of calling them ECOMOG based on their record of operations in Liberia for the past five years. BCADP is interpreted as follows: "B" (be careful) "A" (after) "D" (damaging) "P" (people). BCADP = be careful after damaging the people.

ECOMOG has already damaged Liberia, and then attempts to show love to the Liberians at this time. This is friendship under fire. This also applies to the warring factions as well.

I have pity on the armless, disabled, frustrated women and children who are painfully making friends or even love with these people; just because they have to make a living. I hope their perpetrators will understand that this is not really true love as they pretend. Honest, genuine and peaceful love is never done under fire.

The Creator of all mankind has never supported this type of love and I am certainly sure that God will still not support such today. The theologian says, "Man is a free moral agent to choose his own destiny." I wish that ambitious politicians in Liberia will leave the people in Liberia to decide their own destiny. Put down your guns; let's see who truly loves you.

Stop imposing your ideas of destruction on them under-fire.

FRIENDS OF LIBERIA COMMITMENT TO PEACE NEEDED TO END WAR IN LIBERIA

IN THE YEAR 1994, a concerned group of peace-loving people calling themselves Friends of Liberia, presented a statement explaining their commitment to peace needed to end the Liberian conflict. The statement reads as follows:

In view of escalating levels of fighting and turmoil, and over 150,000 dead, Friends of Liberia calls upon the international community and warring factions to take extraordinary measures to resolve the civil war in Liberia. We appeal to all armed groups to take the first step toward a peaceful resolution of the conflict by agreeing to and abiding by an immediate cease-fire.

The effort to end the conflict has been characterized by a succession of unfulfilled peace agreements. Military factions have splintered. Governments have been changed. Well over a million Liberians have been displaced or made refugees. Yet, hope is still alive among Liberians. The vast majority of Liberians want peace in their nation and a freely elected democratic government. The recently convened Liberia National Conference is representative of this desire. After almost five years of war, the unarmed civilians, tired of being the victims of factional conflict, are trying to take control of their nation's destiny.

The signing of the peace accord at Cotonou, Benin in July 1993 was a positive development that was followed by seven months of negotiation over the make-up of a government. The people of Liberia responded by placing their confidence in the transitional government (LNTG) created by this agreement. The governance provisions of the Cotonou Accord were implemented. What remains unfulfilled is the promise of the armed groups to cease hostilities and disarm.

It is now critical for Liberians, armed and unarmed, to recommit themselves to the Cotonou Agreement for the purpose of securing an immediate cease-fire and disarmament. We plead with the leaders of the various warring factions to set aside self-interest and work toward this goal.

With grave concern about the deterioration of the peace process, we call upon Liberians and the international community to swiftly act upon the following recommendations.

> That the United Nations, together with ECOWAS and the OAU, convene an urgent meeting of all warring factions with discussion focused on achieving a cease-fire and disarmament.
>
> That the warring factions, whether signatory or not to the original agreement, recognize and commit themselves to the Cotonou Agreement.
>
> That all warring factions recognize the Liberia National Transitional Government as the primary governmental authority and support its role in the transition to free and fair elections.
>
> That the nations of the world recognize the sacrifice of ECOWAS and other African countries with peacekeeping forces in Liberia and actively support continuation of their mission.
>
> That all combatants guarantee the safety of innocent civilians, peacekeepers and relief workers.
>
> That U.S. President Bill Clinton appoint a high level presidential adviser for Liberia to emphasize the commitment of the United States of America to lasting peace and effective democracy.

This statement was unanimously adopted by the Board of Trustees of Friends of Liberia at its semi-annual meeting on October 8, 1994.

As Liberia continues to head into a path of death, many peace-loving friends around the world continue to show concern. A genuine letter was addressed to the National Convention in August, 1994; it reads:

Dear People of Liberia,

The 800 members and officers of Friends of Liberia hail the conveeners of the Liberian National Conference. May all participants know that their efforts are apreciated far beyond the borders of the country.

Just as liberty became the symbol of Liberia through her early history, so has the quest for freedom brought you here now from all parts of Liberia. Today you seek freedom from the bonds of war, from the hunger and want that have descended on so many parts of the country, from the fear that rules daily life, from the anger and recrimination that have rekindled the conflict so many times, from the restraints on move-ment and commerce that are reinforced by the divisions among people of this nation.

We extend to you our hopes for success in finding a path to a peaceful future for all the people of Liberia. May this gathering hasten the day when we can all work together to bring the vibrancy back to this nation. Let your initiative be the beginning of a government that will embrace every Liberian and have the rights of individuals as its mandate. We salute you—our friends and neighbors, our students and teachers, our colleagues in planning and growing and building and healing—in this finest hour of your history as you imagine a new life for the nation and the generations who follow you.

Dale Gilles, *Liberia*   Glenn Ivers, *New York*
John Kucij, *New York*   Madeline McMillion, *S.C.*
John Singler, *New York*   Howard Springsteen, *VA*
Julius Walker, D.C.

As these friends of ours continue to show concern and love for Liberia, it becomes our duty to show similar character for this country. The vibrancy which our friends made mention of in their letters to us, can only come through love and oneness. We must keep our hopes alive at all times everywhere in the world for our country of Liberia. We must be dedicated citizens, not gravy-seekers. Liberians are crying everywhere asking themselves, "Why has Liberia become a den of demons? Liberia is a Christian nation as others, has always opened her arms to all for refuge and protection. But, since 1980, demonism has created a high mountain of fear in the minds of all Liberians and friends of Liberia. Before the regime of the late Mr. Samuel Kanyan Doe, Liberia was the home of all Christians and others from all walks of life.

We must return to the real Liberia today; repatriate others from the nation of demons. Liberia is known throughout history as the first Negro Republic in Africa, founded by pioneers from the United States of America; carrying along with them Christian principles which have been practiced in this land for the past one hundred thirty-three years by 1980. Patriotism does not mean to murder other peaceful citizens and encourage others to destroy their own sovereignty, thus inviting foreign dissidents into a peaceful land of liberty.

I become very much shaken, when the warring factions use the words, patriotic and peace. Do they really mean or refer to the actual general definitions of these words, or are they referring to their personal definitions? Because as I can record during Doe's regime, there was a personal dictionary in the Executive Mansion which he oftentime used. The definitions of words from this dictionary did not agree with the general definitions of the same words he often used.

Whenever Mr. Doe said to the nation, "Our soldiers have driven the rebels backward too many miles away from our border," he really meant that the rebels have driven our soldiers many miles into the country. No true patriots will do the things that the warring factions and their loyal troops are doing to the poor Liberian citizens and friends inside Liberia. Patriots do not murder and eat parts of their fellow men whom they protect and defend in time of war.

Who knows his plan?

As I continue to research for this book, I had the opportunity to escort my aunt—Kortoe Jackson—to the U.S. Office of Immigration and Naturalization Services in Arlington, Virginia on January 3, 1996. As the interviewing Asylum Officer opened his interview for which he swore me in to serve as interpreter, his opening statement was, "As far as I am concerned, I do not see nor believe that there will ever be a genuine peace in Liberia—based on the number of peace agreements (60-70) signed and all violated." This was one of the longest interviews ever, said the lawyer of Madame Korto Jackson Sirleaf. A newspaper containing an article entitled, "Fighting Renewed in Liberia," states that there was continued fighting throughout the country again. It maintains that the West African Economic Community Peacekeeping Force

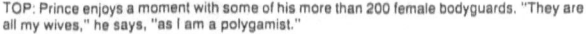

TOP: Prince enjoys a moment with some of his more than 200 female bodyguards. "They are all my wives," he says, "as I am a polygamist."

ABOVE: INPFL fighters. Look at them now, because they may not be around later. Prince has killed a foreigner for giving one of his "wives" a lift, and his own men for stealing one of his Budweisers.

ABOVE RIGHT: One of Prince's young rap revolutionaries waits for something to do with his Browning .50.

MY SERMON FOR JUSTICE

I HAVE PREACHED and continue to preach in the hearing of the people of Liberia to practice justice. It is injustice that has prolonged the Liberian civil crisis. ULIMO came in as a result of injustice. When I was captured by the NPFL forces of Taylor, I saw too many things happen to the Muslims (Mandingos) in Liberia. I saw numerous members of this religion put to death either by firing squad or knives. They were pronounced not important; just as the members of the Krahn tribe were not vital in the Liberian society. I pronounce this act an "INJUSTICE" by the late Samuel Kanyan Doe. Being president of Liberia did not make every Krahn person a president or priviledged character in the country. This is injustice on the part of the doer.

I have lived in the city of Monrovia and other parts of Liberia before and during the crisis. In this respect, my report shall not be limited to any particular region or group specifically. As a matter of fact, communication break down has been one of the major contributing factors to all the atrocities which have taken and are still taking place in Liberia. Therefore, it becomes necessary for any government coming into power in the nation to serve the entire nation in open communication.

Break down of communication in Liberia started when we were yet unborn. The past governments had always failed to disseminate necessary, needed information in the hearing of the citizens. With the assumption that they were not necessary for everybody but only the ruling few, forgetting to realize that the common people are in the majority; hence, their uprising could cause serious damage to the national government. In this connection, there existed very little understanding between the common people and the national government.

Having said that, a very heavy uprising arose among the entire citizenry on several instances where some people lost their lives instantly. On one particular occasion, April 14, 1979, there was serious political unrest in the city of Monrovia during the late President William Richard Tolbert Jr.'s administration led by one Mr. G. Baccus Matthews. This political unrest claimed the lives of some citizens and a great quantity of properties. But the late Tolbert's administration did not consider this as a threat to the government. Rather thought that he (Tolbert) could easily place the situation under control without any harm to the nation; information was poorly disseminated, not as expected by the Liberians. Therefore, Mr. Matthews and his collaborators used this error on the part of the administration as gross negligence and also used it as loop-holes for them to destabilize the genuine peace and stability of the country. One philosopher once said, "Communication is the matter of understanding."

Definitely, if you cannot understand people, you can never freely communicate with them at any level. Many organizations, associations, families and most importantly, national governments have fallen apart due to lack of or poor communications; failure on the parts of leaders to disseminate information in the hearing of their members or citizens as needed.

Failure to disseminate information creates an atmosphere of rumor (talk or opinion widely disseminated with no discernible source) which often-time creates chaos.

Secrecy is one of the most dangerous tools which any leadership can use. Once these characters are created in the minds of others, the leadership is bound to fall.

It creates an atmosphere of distrust, and misbelief. A husband or wife must create an atmosphere of trust, confidence, sincerity, honesty and belief. The best thing any married couple could possibly do whenever disbelief, distrust and lack of sincere confidence enters their married life is to separate. When a leader finds himself going down-hill due to those above mentioned characteristics, he or she must be smart enough to understand that it is time to step down.

The worst and perhaps most damaging method a leader can ever use is threat (an expression of intention to inflict evil, injury or damage) against his or her people. Today, there are wars, rumors of wars, subsequently, coups d'etat in Africa everywhere on the continent because of "Injustice," protected by threat. Break down of communication has again created serious problems in the Liberian crisis. It can be recorded that several agreements have been signed to no avail due to the misunderstandings I suppose. See the Akosombo Agreement.

This Agreement on the clarification of the Akosombo Agreement made this 21st day of December A.D. 1994 is intended to clarify and expand pertinent provisions of the said Akosombo Agreement.

SECTION A

ARTICLE 1
CEASE FIRE

The Parties to this Agreement hereby declare a Cease Fire and the cessation of hostilities effective as of 23:59 hours (11:59 pm) on the 28th day of December 1994.

SECTION C

ARTICLE 4
TERMS AND CONDITIONS
(SAFE HAVENS AND BUFFER ZONES)

Consistent with Section C Article 4 count 5 of the Akosombo Agreement, the parties agree to facilitate the establishment of Safe Havens and Buffer Zones throughout Liberia in accordance with a plan to be drawn up by the LTNG in collaboration with UNOMIL and ECOMOG in consultation with the parties. In this connection, the Council of State established under the Akosombo Agreement clarified by this agreement shall establish appropriate committees which will be charged with determining the criteria for recruitment, taking advantage of the relevant expertise of ECOMOG and UNOMIL.

SECTION H

ARTICLE 9
DEMOBILIZATION

Consistent with Section H Article 9 count 4 of the Akosombo Agreement, it is agreed by the parties that in the reorganization of the Armed Forces of Liberia, the Police, Immigration and other Security Agencies, the combatants and non-combatants who satisfy conditions for recruitment shall be considered for inclusion. In this connection, the Council of State established under the Akosombo Agreement, taking advantage of the relevant expertise of ECOMOG and UNOMIL.

SECTION K

ARTICLE 12
SCHEDULE OF IMPLEMENTATION

The parties hereby agree to abide by the schedule of implementation hereto attached and incorporated herein by reference.

PART II
POLITICAL ISSUES

SECTION A

(EXECUTIVE)

Consistent with Part II Section A (i), of the Akosombo Agreement the provision for the function and structure of the Five-Member Council of State provided for in the Cotonou and Akosombo Agreements are hereby reconfirmed.

The procedure for the appointment of the relevant officials of government as enshrined in the Akosombo Agreement is hereby reaffirmed.

Such officials shall be appointed based on merit. The parties agree that a five-member council of state shall be established.

The first four members of the new council of state shall be appointed as follows:

NPFL...1
ULIMO 1
AFL. COALITION 1
LNC 1

The fifth member of the council of state shall be a traditional chief selected by the NPFL and ULIMO in person of Honourable Tamba Tailor in accordance with Part II Section A (i) of the Akosombo Agreement and agreed, by the parties. Consistent with Part II Section A (i) of the Akosombo Agreement, induction of the council of state shall take place in the city of Monrovia under the auspices of the Chairman of ECOMAS or his designee within fourteen (14) days as of the cease fire date.

SECTION H

ARTICLE 20

Consistent with Article 20 of the Akosombo Agreement, the parties reaffirm the acceptance of the ECOWAS Peace Plan including the Cotonou AND Akosombo Agreements as the best framework for peace in Liberia.

In spite of this Agreement and many others, the warring factions continue to fight and butcher as many peaceful, helpless citizens as they can in Liberia. Communication is still a major problem in the nation today. Today, we are still looking forward to an improvement in our communication skills in Liberia.

TAYLOR AGREES

Mr. Charles G. Taylor, the leader of the National Patriotic Front of Liberia, agreed for the 1995 and the preparations for the general elections from June 8 to November 11. The election was scheduled to be held on November 14, 1995 while the inauguration of the new government would take place in January of the following year, 1996 respectively.

The leaders of the seven warring factions, including AFL, NPFL, ULIMO K, CRC NPFL, ULIMO J, LDF, and LPC, signed the agreement on Wednesday at a brief ceremony in the Ghanaian capital, Accra. The signing was done in the presence of ECOWAS' Chairman, Mr. John Jerry Rawlings, the ex-president of Zimbabwe and OAU eminent person on Liberia, the Rev. Dr. Cannan Banana and nine West African foreign ministers.

The agreement is a clarification of the Akosombo Accord, a portion of which was rejected by four of the seven factions who were not signatories to the document initially signed in mid-September.

You may observe that some of the major points in the agreement include the establishment of ceasefire which was due to come into effect December 28, 1995; a new five-men council of state which will be installed within (14) days of the ceasefire date.

According to reports from the talks, the NPFL, ULIMO, and the Liberia National Conference, the Armed Force of Liberia and the Coalition will share a seat while a traditional chief chosen by ULIMO and NPFL in the person of chief Tamba Taylor will be given a seat.

Meanwhile, the leader of the National Patriotic Front of Liberia, Mr. Charles G. Taylor, also agreed to disarm his Forces to the multi-national West African Peace Monitoring group, ECOMOG.

Mr. Taylor made the disclosure the next day in an interview with a BBC news reporter. He said that the AFL, ULIMO, and NPFL on Wednesday signed a non-aggression pact. He noted that they were of the belief that their action would go a long way in encouraging others to follow what they have done.

On his coming to Monrovia, Mr. Taylor said he expects to be in Monrovia for the seating of the new government soon. However, he did not indicate date nor time. Though he seems to have accepted and acknowledged all the agreements and the common understandings thereto, it can be recorded that Mr. Taylor's fighting and constant attacks did not seem to end.

Mr. Taylor said that most of his attacks on his enemies were based on the disadvantages taken over his position as a patriotic leader of the common people. In that light, he was obligated to defend and protect the rights of his people at all times. Following his statement closely, it was observed and noted by me during the writing of this book, that while Mr. Taylor was on a peace mission in the Ghanaian capital, Accra 1994, his territory of Bong County and his stronghold of Gbarnga city were attacked by the ULIMO forces of Mr. Kroma, demoralizing Gbarnga city and completely destroying Mr. Taylor's living quarters.

This left Mr. Taylor with no other alternative but to continue his usual aggressive attacks on ULIMO upon his return from Ghana. Mr. Kroma, who claims to be for the common Liberian people, has done more harm to them than good. Under his command, too many villages were wiped out along with thousands of the inhabitants. I pray and hope that Mr. Kroma doesn't come to my rescue in the future.

LIBERIANS MUST SAVE THEMSELVES

When the OAU eminent person on the Liberian conflict, Rev. Cannan Banana addressed the Liberia National Conference in August 1994, he told the delegates that the country was at the crossroad of life and death and urged all Liberians to choose the paths that lead to life instead of those that lead to death and destruction. Many of the flowery and beautiful speeches delivered there have either been forgotten or overwhelmed by the flurry of events taking place in the country.

But that message of Rev. Banana still rings in the ears of all Liberians and their minds since the close of that conference. Or, better still, his short and sincere message should guide us (Liberians) in our search for genuine peace.

There is no question we as a nation are on the crossroads of life and death. The entire Liberian nation is rapidly moving on the path of death and self-destruction while those who should salvage the situation continuously demonstrate a lack of commitment and sincerity when it comes to the peace process.

As a result of renewed hostilities, hundreds of our people are dying of hunger and disease in the Southeastern, Central and other parts of the country while our warlords, the Liberians, the patriots and the defenders look on with selfish ambition and pride.

In short, he said Liberians, particularly the key players, have failed to allow reason to prevail and thus save their dying and war-ravaged country.

In the face of all these negative developments at home, the international community, our extreme partners, are growing impatient with the general attitudes toward peace. Numerous peace accords have been signed and reneged upon while scarce resources have been wasted to assist us out of this mess that we are in.

We hope that all is now approaching an end. An end which could be for us or against our destiny as a nation, depending on which way we choose to go. The United Nations was about to cut down on its present force of about 300 to less than 100. In addition to the United Nations' decision, the West African Peace-Keeping Force (ECOMOG) was to reduce its strength shortly because of its financially constrained lack of logistics in Liberia on the very ground in need. The overall economic effects of the operation on the countries contributing troops in the Republic of Liberia were faced with numerous difficulties.

Already, Liberians and foreign residents have begun growing nervous as a result of the latest developments. But, as we have always said, "others can help us, but the responsibility to restore peace rests with Liberians themselves." So let us, especially the warring factions and key players, measure up to the challenge and save ourselves.

According to the international monetary funds (IMF) and World Bank annual report conference held October, 1994, Liberia should have learned a lesson, but she hasn't. This conference could best be described as another scene of the revival of the North-South split of the 1910s representing different economic interests. Had the request for additional Special Drawing Rights (SDR) from finance ministers of the developing countries gone well with their counterparts of the seven industrial nations, perhaps there could have been a transfer of financial resources to the developing countries of the South region.

If you take a keen look at it from this point or stated position, the rejection of the process proposal and exclusion of the South by the seven industrial nations finance ministers from receiving the SDR option offered to Russia and other central and eastern European countries did not represent the economic interest of countries in the South.

One can clearly see that, in the rebirth of old rivalry, perhaps the South saw the North dominating its interest again. And that might have caused the South's finance ministers to even term the decision of their counterparts as "too mean."

However, this 1994 annual conference of the IMF and the World Bank held in early October in Madrid, Spain, climaxed with a dialogue between finance ministers of both developing and industrial nations for new credit limits represent SDR under the fund. The North should have put up $50 billion of SDR for future new credit purposes if a deal had been struck between the North and South economic regions. Russia and the rest of the world countries of central and eastern Europe could have benefited as well.

Unfortunately, the North's finance ministers rejected this proposal and offered $20 billion. They excluded countries of the South.

According to observations and developments leading to the Madrid meeting, this moment in the conference could represent changing of views within the IMF and the World Bank about the option between the fund and Bank's own lending and private financial market that can speed up the economic reform process going on in the developing countries. Giving $50 billion could have just been seen by the North as working against their private investors' interest in the IMF structural adjustment program (SAP) for the emerging markets and assets it creates. This also goes for the Fund and the Bank intiatives in this regard to have economic reform in the South.

When the Bank published its annual report this year, it observed that developing countries' economics received much more finance from the private financial markets. That in itself is a tacit approval of this development. The Bank also supports development and growth of the emerging markets with establishment of funds such as $50 million of George Soros' Quantum Funds of $200 million, and $30 million Africa Fund under the Emerging Markets Investment Corporation (EMIC).

What this says for the rest of Africa and Liberia in particular is that these countries will have to go through more of the economic reforms that have cut down public sectors' sizes in other emerging market's economies and increase private sectors' holding of production resources for the fund and Bank assistance. The IMF SAP usually makes way for these reforms in order to have the market where state enterprises' stocks and government debts are traded.

Liberia's future SAP could be for the country to undergo privatization and government debt liquidation that could bring debt relief from the sales of state-owned enterprises' assets arranged under the Africa Fund.

THE INTERNATIONAL RESPONSE:

Human rights guarantees have not been a part of the ECOWAS effort in Liberia, which has focused exclusively on peace. The only ECOWAS document that even mentioned human rights concerns was published in November 1992, when the communique of the ECOWAS summit in Abuja stated that "Heads of State and Governments, in the face of mounting evidence of atrocities, warned all warring factions against the commission of war crimes and crimes against humanity in Liberia."

On October 20 in Cotonou, Benin, the ECOWAS standing Mediation Committee and the Committee of Five decided to impose sanctions "against any party to the Liberian conflict which fails to comply with the implementation of the Yamoussoukro IV Accord, and in particular the National Patriotic Front of Liberia (NPFL), led by Charles Taylor." Were these actions on the part of the Committees justifiable, when they were particularly limited to one specific party to the conflict? These sanctions prevented the export of any weapons or military equipment; the import or export of commodities and products to or from NPFL controlled territory; and access to or from Liberia for persons and vehicles "except for strictly humanitarian purposes."

Did this rule apply to all parties to the conflict, or just to NPFL alone? The sanctions were imposed following the November 7 ECOWAS Committee of Nine meeting in Abuja, Nigeria. In addition to renewing its call for a cease-fire, the meeting asked the U.N.'s Secretary General to appoint a Special Representative for Liberia. The U.N. Security Council was asked to endorse the ECOWAS sanctions decision.

The ECOWAS leaders met in Abuja, Nigeria, on November 7, and issued a communique calling for a cease-fire effective midnight November 10, and the subsequent encampment and disarmament of all warring parties; the appointment by the Secretary General of the United Nations of a Special Representative to help implement the ECOWAS peace plan, and the imposition of sanctions.

The question is, was ECOWAS seriously monitoring the activities of ECOMOG in Liberia as it should, especially the continued human rights abuses, among other things?

ECOWAS seems to be stepping up its effort to block cross-border humanitarian assistance to NPFL territory where the bulk of the population resides from the Ivory Coast areas. It was very good for ECOWAS to show such a concern, but what about the other sides of the conflict? In early May, 1993, ECOWAS Executive Secretary Abass Bundu called on relief organizations to cease all cross-border relief operations and announced the establishment of a "tranquility corridor" through which relief supplies would be transported, policed by ECOMOG.

Mr. Taylor strongly opposes such a plan. ECOMOG contends that Mr. Taylor uses the cross-border convoys to transport supplies for his forces, and has told relief organizations that they must inform ECOMOG when they conduct cross-border operations. (The fact that MSF did not inform ECOMOG about its convoy in April is believed to have prompted the ECOMOG air strike on the convoy.) However, humanitarian aid is exempt from the U.N. embargo of November, 1992, and ECOWAS's stand contradicts the U.N.'s mandate to deliver such assistance.

These latest efforts to curtail the delivery of humanitarian assistance are very disturbing. Reports indicate that ECOMOG will consider any relief operations coming from the Ivorian border to be a legitimate target. According to a May 19 press release issued by the Liberian mission to the United Nations, ECOMOG has issued an ominous warning:

While it is part of ECOMOG's reponsibility to support the supply of relief materials to every part of Liberia, it has the right, through its peace enforcement mandate, to determine the easiest and safest corridor through which to achieve this objective. Therefore, ECOMOG will not accept any activity that will render it incapable of fulfilling its mandate and expose it and peaceful citizens to danger. ECOMOG warned that no relief agency or NGO has any right to impede the efforts of ECOMOG in its peace enforcement mission.

THE UNITED NATIONS

Although the United Nations has contributed significantly to the emergency relief and humanitarian aid that has gone to Liberia, the United Nations did not address the Liberian crisis in political terms until November 1992, almost three years after the crisis erupted. All indications are that the United Nations considers Liberia a regional problem best dealt with by ECOWAS, the regional body. The U.N.'s emphasis has been to shift responsibility to the ECOWAS. "Boutros Ghali is adamant that ECOMOG works out," commented a former U.N. employee. While strengthening and supporting the regional organization is a laudable effort, the U.N. should ensure that human rights issues figure prominently in the regional organization's efforts and that the organization itself does not contribute to aggravating the war. In this respect, the United Nations' record in Liberia is poor compared to Liberia's membership record as one of the founding member countries.

In fact, the promotion and protection of human rights has become part of the United Nations' efforts at conflict resolution in other parts of the world. Human rights issues have figured prominently in U.N. brokered agreements in such diverse places as El Salvador, Cambodia and Haiti. The U.N. should apply some of that experience to Liberia.

It is ironic that the secretary general's report on Liberia in March 1993 cites Liberia as an example of "systematic cooperation between the United Nations and a regional organization, as envisaged in Chapter VIII of the Charter." In fact, the U.N. has been largely absent and is seeking to distance itself from any commitment to protecting human rights in Liberia.

On November 19, the United Nations Security Council adopted resolution 188, calling on all parties to the conflict to respect a cease-fire and authorize an arms embargo against Liberia. The ECOMOG force is exempt from the embargo, subject to future review. The Security Council resolution also requested the secretary general to send a special representative to Liberia to evaluate the situation and report back to the Secretary Council. The special representative, Trevor Livingston Gordon-Somers, who works for the United Nations Development Program (UNDP), was appointed the following day, and visited the region in November-December 1992, January to February 1993, and April 1993.

LIBERIA:
CONTINUING TO DRIFT

A Speech by Dr. Joseph G. Morris on the occasion of Liberia's 147th
Anniversary of Independence
Baltimore, Maryland, United States of America

MY FELLOW LIBERIANS and friends of Liberia, greetings from your
fellow Liberians in Indianapolis, Indiana. We are meeting here today to
observe the 147th anniversary of our nation's Independence. Significantly,
we are doing so at a time when that nation continues to bleed and agonize
from a brutal and devastating civil war.

I do not need to remind you how destructive, traumatic and demoralizing
that has been for our nation and its people. But let me borrow a few words from
a report submitted to the United States Senate by Senator Edward Kennedy,
Chairman of the sub-committee on Immigration and Refugee Affairs of the
United States Senate to give you a sense of how he saw it in 1991.

"The war has resulted in the largest per capita displacement of refugees
in any country in the world today—more than 1.2 million persons out of an
estimated 2.5 million population have been displaced from their homes and
lands; as many as 730,000 have fled the country, while another estimated
1.2 million are displaced . . . more than 10,000 persons have died . . ."

The estimate I saw some three months ago put the number of dead at
more than 30,000, and fighting continues, although at a reduced level.

My dear friends, ever since the founding of the Liberian nation through
the instrumentality of the American Colonization Society, the assistance
and encouragement of the Government of the United States and the Kings
and Chiefs of the territory which is now Liberia, the nation has moved

from one crisis to another, but has always sustained the will to survive. The path has not always been smooth, but the people have been relentless in their determination to succeed. Unfortunately, the Liberian civil war has changed all of that.

On an occasion like this, it is incumbent on Liberians everywhere to reflect on the nation, mourn the dead, lament the loss, the horror, the atrocities, the devastation, and the agony this brutal war has brought upon our nation. In this hour of grief, let our hearts yearn for the opportunity to return home, pick up the pieces, put our lives together, and rebuild the nation. And, as we contemplate the rebuilding process, we invite our friends and traditional partners in progress to lend us a helping hand. Of course, partnership in development is not strange to the lovely people of Baltimore. And I shall return to this later.

Today, as we observe our national day, let our observance assume the character of reflection—reflect on the recent past, assess the present, and chart a course of action for the future, particularly the future of our nation and children. Our recent past should inspire us to keep hope alive. Thus, we should remember that Liberia, although small in size, is rich in natural resources—human and material. In agriculture, the country has a large amount of land well-suited for growing export-oriented tree crops, particularly rubber, coffee, cocoa, oil palms, coconuts as well as for domestic consumption. Mineral resources consist of iron ore, diamonds and gold. The iron ore deposits were of major importance, with output substantially increasing from 3.1 million long tons in 1960 to 15.9 million long tons in 1965 and 21.1 million long tons in 1969. Liberia became the world's eleventh largest producer of iron ore.

Rubber production both by concessions and Liberian planters also rose immensely, accounting for 38 percent and 17 percent, respectively, of total monetary GDP.

Liberia's rapid economic growth continued in the decade of the 1970's, showing estimated per capita GDP of $2,400 for the enclave's economy and nearly $900 for the national monetary economy.

During the early 1970's, mining accounted for some 31 percent of total GDP, declining to about 21 percent in the mid-1970's. Mining's share rose again in 1980-1981, but drastically declined in 1982-1983. Iron ore, gold, and diamonds were economically significant in 1984. Other minerals located, but not considered profitably exploitable by mid-1984, include barite, bauxite, clay ilmenite, rutile, heavy sand deposits of chromite, copper, lead, zinc, columbite-tantalite, maganese, tin and tungsten.

MANUFACTURING

Manufacturing is small and in its infancy. Focus is mainly on such items as cement, bricks, cement tiles and blocks, wooden and metal furniture, household goods, clothing, etc.

The economy is based on the "free enterprise" concept and the monetary system on the United States dollar.

On the political front, successive, entrenched, minority-dominated oligarchy held power too long, resulting in a frustrated majority, resentful of their systematic exclusion from meaningful participation in the democratic process at the highest level of decision making in government. While the minority-dominated contemporary True Whig Party Governments of Tubman and Tolbert realized the political and economic disparity in the Liberian society and tried to address it, they were creatures of a system which frustrated their efforts.

The 1980 military coup, led by Master Sergeant Samuel Kanyon Doe was, in my opinion, a response to the insensitivity of the ruling class to the plight of the masses, while the on-going civil war appears, to some extent, a follow-up of the process. One would have thought that with the death of Doe and the collapse of his government, the objective of the National Patriotic Front of Liberia, which was to remove Doe from power, would have been met, and steps taken to establish a truly democratic government through free and fair democratic elections.

But the fact that this has not happened is a reasonable basis to speculate that those who sought to remove Doe from power might have had other hidden agenda. Meanwhile, Liberia continued to drift. Now, let me return to the Gbarnga-Baltimore Sister-City Relationship.

The Gbarnga-Baltimore Sister-City Relationship is a true expression of partnership in development and a vehicle for the promotion of cross-cultural understanding. The "Welcome Reception for The Honourable James D. Norris, Mayor," of the City of Gbarnga, Bong County, hosted by the Gbarnga-Baltimore Sister City Committee recently in this great city is testimony to the mutually rewarding nature of this venture and the benefits that can accrue to both parties, if properly implemented. And those individuals who have been responsible for directing and implementing this joint venture here and in Gbarnga deserve highest commendation. However, if ever there was a need to accentuate and upgrade this relationship, it is now, because the civil war has added new urgency to the objectives envisaged by this venture.

Gbarnga is an innocent victim of the civil war by serving as head-quarters of Charles Taylor's National Patriotic Front Movements even though not by choice. This situation exposed our little city and its inhabitants to sustained attacks and air bombardments by ECOMOG forces, resulting in severe damage and destruction to the already inadequate infrastructures of the city. The population also suffered—those unable to flee, died. The children, too, were not spared—the unfortunate ones, perished, others were traumatized.

Forcibly enlisted in the rebel army (some of them as young as twelve), they were manipulated and programmed to kill. Thus, guns replaced textbooks in the hands of thousands of these children; love, trust and confidence were replaced by hate, fear and suspicion. School buildings and campuses were converted to military use. The only hospital, Phebe, under-staffed, under-supplied and ill-equipped, is crammed with the sick and the wounded, both military and civilian.

A post civil war Gbarnga-Baltimore Sister-City Venture might want to take a look at the plight of these children who are calling out for rehabilitation, encouragement and support; children, many of whom have become orphans overnight; children whose lives have been shattered, children who have lost hope.

The urgency of this matter lies in the fact that, even before the civil war, education was a major problem for the Liberian government. All efforts to provide basic, elementary education for all children was impossible, and rural children were particularly at a disadvantage. And the civil war has compounded the problem.

Let me conclude by appealing to the warring parties to give the Liberian people a "26" present—peace of mind and hope. Give the Liberian people an opportunity to decide through the ballot box, who should lead them in a post-civil war Liberia. What they need now is an internationally supervised, democratic election. Let the warring parties give democracy a chance.

Finally, I salute Bong Kwoe Association for organizing this program and inviting me to participate in it. I congratulate and thank the Gbarnga-Baltimore Sister-City Committee for their sustained interest in the people of Bong County. I appeal to the committee to continue its efforts, I appreciate the opportunity to visit Baltimore once more.

SOME OF THE MAJOR CAUSES OF THE LIBERIAN CIVIL WAR

THE COMING IN and going out of the Progressives of the (PRC) Government of the late president Samuel K. Doe. How Mr. Chea and Oscar were dropped out of the limelight, the leader attempted putting termed a "brilliant idea" on the part of the leader and often times was subsequently fired, but never discharged from the army.

His comrades, Togba, George and Boima, never uttered a word or even prevailed on the leader to rescind his decision in accordance with the art of diplomacy, which calls for continuity, failing to rethink the adage of old, which states that town trap is not for rats alone. But before all of this could happen, Togba, who was appointed to a ministerial position just as his comrades, was responsible to draw up an economic policy to improve the living standard of the people, which was only cosmetic, as the main forum behind the drive was to win public confidence for the PRC.

So Togba went about doing his homework, and a few days later came out with a pronouncement that the PRC had only US $5 million in the national coffers.

He told the nation that although there was no money, the PRC, in the cause of the people, had decided to raise civil servants pay by 100 percent.

At the time some employees in the public sector were earning far less than US $200, but at the Foreign their needs were being met.

No sooner had the PRC increased salaries in the public sector when, months later, all kinds of taxes, including development and reconstruction, social security, as well as the savings bond scheme, were affected, thereby reducing civil servants pay to less than they were previously earning.

When all became well for the leader, he concocted plans to get rid of Togba, one of the remaining three progressives left in the PRC government.

And so, Togba was asked to resign or be sacked. I really don't know what transpired between him and the leader. While out of the country, he was implicated in a coup plot to topple the leader.

At this time, Boima, who had replaced Gabriel at the Foreign Ministry, along with George and Doupu, were faring well with the leader.

Boima had used his socialist influence to have some 66 Liberians sent to Ethiopia to undergo a literacy training program in a bid to help eliminate the high rate of illiteracy in the country during the regime of the PRC.

By this time, Oscar had been replaced by Edward while Isaac had taken over from Chea. Bernie was sent in the foreign service as Liberia's Ambassador accredited to the Holy Land of Israel. Albert, who replaced him, did not last any longer, as Gray, who served as Information Minister at this time, took over the Defense Ministry as Minister. Now the Animal Farm had entered its second stage; with the leader consolidating his position by replacing the Progression with key officials who had served the previous regime, as a sign of reconciliation. Lest I forget, Mrs. Ellen Johnson Sirleaf, a prominent female banker, was also appointed by the leader to serve as president of the Liberia Bank for Development and Investment. She later abandoned the job for greener pastures in the United States.

Now the time was ripe to kick out the last Progressives from the PRC and so the leader called in his master planners to concoct a scheme to get rid of Boima, while at the same time not leaning on the progressives too hard. Then Isaac, the leader's legal arm, along with Gray, came up with a plan that Boima, unknowing to the government, had sent some 66 Liberians including the present Assistant Sports Minister.

These saboteurs, as the 66 were referred to by the government, were expected in the country to topple the government, and the security forces were on the alert. They later returned and some of them were rounded up for questioning, but later released because the state could not prove its case, just as it has been in too many accused cases by the government.

The Animal Farm was by then entering stage three of the elimination process of the progressives. All of the progressives who had made a lot of noise in the Tolbert regime had now tasted state power, but their performances were rated unsatisfactorily by the leader, who now desired to mingle with men of the old order, to at least appease prominent Liberians, who had fled the country during the coup, to return and help put the country back on course.

Doupu, too, was sacked as a labor minister and later implicated in the Nimba raid of 1983. Charles Taylor, now the NPFL leader, one of the Progressives at the time, and a favorite of the leader was paradoxically now appointed Director-General of the General Services Agency (GSA), a junior cabinet position he held from 1980-1982.

The fast-talking wheeler-dealer politely moved into the GSA Compound on April 20 and took over, using his influence to acquire 17 mini Hondas for the PRC members, a move that helped Charles to be commissioned a Major in the Armed Forces of Liberia just like the Cabinet Ministers, an action which indicated that anyone could become a highranking official in this government once you do something which favors the leader.

The leader then began to admire Charles, the only Director-General at the time who was allowed to attend cabinet meetings.

Then Charles decided to centralize all government purchases under the bulk purchasing scheme. After much maneuvering, the PRC finally approved the scheme and Charles was now buying everything needed by the various ministries and agencies to make them functional.

A product of the old order, Charles, who hailed from Arthington Montserrado County, gradually gained prominence through his flamboyant behavior, and his ability to get things going.

As a reporter of the new Liberian Newspaper indicated to me, Ministry of Information, the GSA was a routine beat, and after publishing a series of stories on efforts being made by the GSA to reduce spending through cost-saving measures, six-door seated Mercedes Benz (black) and gray used by President William V. S. Tubman, for some US $500,000 to win the heart of the leader.

After he had done all of this in the four years he ran the GSA controlling millions of dollars, the leader decided that Charles and Clarence should swap positions.

Clarence was a Deputy Minister at the Commerce Ministry, and this annoyed Charles Taylor who had built up an effective system to the extent that government could credit anything from any of its vendors without any problem. And so, in a bid not to raise suspicion, Charles took over from Clarence and was welcomed on board by McLeod, who too was a Deputy Minister there.

Charles knew that his time with the leader was running short as his removal from the GSA indicated his slow decline from grace to grass. He then asked the leader for permission to seek medical treatment abroad as he had been afflicted with small pox.

The leader, who apparently had something up his sleeve for Charles, did not readily agree. However, some other members of the PRC, who were friends of Charles and knew exactly what was being planned, helped him to get out of the country through the Ivory Coast. However, prior to his departure, Charles was being audited by the Bureau of General Audits.

As soon as the leader heard that Charles had fled, he announced that the latter had duped government of millions through the bulk purchasing scheme and had set up a fictitious earth moving company in the United States in collaboration with the Dillion Brothers, who previously had their store on the UN Drive, through which funds were siphoned from the state coffers.

This, then, closed the chapter of the Progressives, as the leader now consolidated his position, by bringing in men of the old order to appease prominent Liberians, most of whom were members of the TWP, but were now residing in the United States.

The Liberian civil war has created a series of problems; such as grief, mourning, bereavement, etc. However, we are going to address each of these situations separately.

What is grief? It is defined as the process of working through a loss. It consists of four specific phases: to accept the loss, to experience the pain, to adjust the environment without the one who has died, and to reinvest energy into other relationships.

Mourning is the process of letting go. This is the stage which too many people cannot withstand.

Bereavement is defined as the awareness of experience of loss.

According to Dr. Arnoldo Fangrazzi, writing in Catholic Update, there are ten suggestions to help overcome grief: take time to accept the death—facing and accepting death remains a necessary condition for continuing our own life. Take time to let go—letting go means adjusting to a new reality in which the deceased is no longer present. Letting go occurs when we are able to accept whatever feelings—anger, guilt, fear, sadness—accompanying death. Letting go occurs when we are able to tolerate the feelings, to wait, trust and hope again. Take time to make decisions—it is important that the bereaved be patient with himself and gradually make decisions as a way to control and sustain self worth. But it is wise to postpone major decisions.

Take time to share—the greatest need of the bereaved is to have someone share his pain, his memories, his sadness. Take time to believe—for many people, religion offers a comforting and strengthening base in the lonely encounter with helplessness and hopelessness. Take time to forgive—we need to accept our imperfections, not torture ourselves for the things we did or did not do. Take time to meet new friends—healing occurs when we move out of our safe boundaries and interact with others. New friends will be there to offer opportunities. Join a support group, a club or take a class.

Take time to laugh—laughter helps us survive and re-enter life. Take time to give—the best way to overcome loneliness and grief is to be concerned about the pain of others.

If we find someone who needs us, that will be our opportunity for healing. Get involved with others. Take time to feel good about yourself—exploring new interests, developing hobbies and taking advantage of new opportunities are all activities designed to help the bereaved reinvest his energies in new endeavors. Take time to meet new friends—healing occurs when we move out of our safe boundaries and interact with others.

How will one know that he or she is feeling better, or do you know that you are feeling better too? Although it is believed that everybody has her/his own style and timeline of grief, you can easily measure your progress by certain feelings and behaviors which come about as you feel better. As your sense of humor returns, and you find yourself laughing, you know you are now feeling better. As you find your mood swings between so high and so low, you can feel the time lengthen between upsets.

When you hear yourself giving some human qualities to your deceased loved one as you recall past moments, then you know you are moving through the worst of your grief. As you find yourself making major decisions, you take responsibility for determining the quality of your life . . . you are feeling better.

When you are making new friends, you insure that you will have supportive people around you in the future and seldom have to be lonely. Finally, when you learn that your life is in your hands and that you are capable of taking charge, you will know that you are truly growing.

The situation in Liberia today has created and continues more and worse creation than ever before in the past. If not all citizens and residents of Liberia, 99% of them are going through the aforementioned stages. Hereafter, they shall continue to undergo same. Then the question comes, who do we need to help us to be able to cope with this situation? It is true that we obviously need the Most High, the Creator—God. But, in any case, God uses human beings to carry out His wishes. In this light, we will surely need some qualified persons to deal wiith the situation.

As a citizen and an author of Liberia, I will strongly suggest that the nation employ the services of some experts in the form of scientists, psychologists, sociologists, anthropologists, medical doctors, lawyers, engineers and theologians.

These people, with their professional knowledge together with their experience, could possibly be able to deal with the dying nation's problems and its people, not forgetting to mention that educators and educationists are seriously needed in such a process. We are aware that they will face the worst problems. Why, because the youths of Liberia have been wrongfully and dangerously misled and miseducated by men of evil minds. In this regard, the educators will have to uneducate them first, and then re-educate them rightfully. Therefore, it is not an easy job for them in the entire rebuilding process. Thereby, we need men and women who will be trained and surely ready to exercise a great deal of patience.

WAR/CIVIL WAR

IF I ASK ANYONE to rightfully define the word war, there will be a series of both personal and general definitions. As a matter of fact, war is one of the most critical situations in the life of mankind, if not the only one. There are numerous types of wars in our world today.

Today, the world is faced with a great bundle of catastrophe everywhere. War, by definition, is a strife, to confuse, a state of usual open and declared armed hostile conflict between states or nations, a state between opposing forces or for a particular end. A state of hostility, conflict, antagonism; a state of struggle or competition between opposing forces for a specific end. In the Great United States of America, the war of "drug abusers" is very serious indeed, hundreds and thousands of kids, youths as well as adults, lose their lives each and every year. This is a God-blessed nation among other nations in our world today. Even in the homes, there is war being fought between the husband and wife, children and parents.

Families are fighting wars as well, community against community, human beings against disease, disease against human beings. But, to what end are they all? As the philosopher once said, "The end justifies the means." I will define CIVIL WAR as husband against his wife and children in that he will be responsible to restore and rebuild whatever atrocities he brought on himself, regretting thereafter. In this instance, I look at civil war as an inferior and idiotic situation. Liberians are responsible to rebuild and restore whatsoever materials they themselves have destroyed and then grieve for their loved ones whom they themselves have caused or contributed to their lives lost. What sense have they then? I am in sympathy with those who claim innocence on the premises. On the contrary, I am angry with those who created the situation. What are they doing about the situation created by them? Are they helping to resolve the problem, or continuing to make the situation worse? These people have brought into the country civil war; will they help to bring in civil rights?

In order for a country to better survive from the atrocities of a civil war, there must follow the creation of civil rights.

THE SOLUTION OF OUR PROBLEMS

If Liberians ever needed unity at home and abroad, now is the time; with mutual understanding. With love, peace of mind, sincerity, honesty, humbleness and dedication, Liberians can possibly find solutions to their problems.

With this in mind, the Liberian community in Baltimore, Maryland U.S.A., gathered together on December 17, 1994 at the All Saints Lutheran Church to discuss and plan some important strategies which would be of help to the Liberians at home and abroad. Here is a copy of their resolutions prepared on that day:

CONSULTATIVE CONFERENCE OF
THE LIBERIAN PEOPLE

17 DECEMBER 1994

THE UNITED VOICE OF LIBERIA

1. The conference shall agree on the urgent need for Liberian unity and pledges itself to work for it on the basis of the following broad principles:

    a. The immediate removal of the scourge of warlord factions from every phase of national life in Liberia.
    b. The immediate resotration of peace and democracy in Liberia.
    c. The effective use of non-violent pen pressures against warlord factions.

2. This conference of Liberian people from all walks of life, having carefully studied and examined the grave problems of Liberia, our country, will place on record that:

    a. It is convinced that the continual absenteeism of the true practice of the fundamental rights and in particular, the right to have freedom of movement and expression or the press which went on rampantly in Liberia for one hundred and thirty-three years, was responsible for the 1980 coup d'etat which has finally resulted in civil war, which has created massive destructions, sectional and tribal tensions and persistent conflict in our country.

b.   It is its considered view that the situation is further aggrevated by the efforts of the warlord factions to muzzle the democratic peace expression of the people of Liberia by continued disruption of the process.

c.   There is no doubt that the creation of a new organization for a democratic peace restoration, unity with contemptuous regard for the view of the Liberian people is a climax in this determining process.

d.   This conference shall note with concern that the developments in Liberia are dramatically opposed to those in or have taken place in the rest of Africa—wherefore, conference warns that the situation in our country has created an atmosphere charged with the possibility of a continual massacre unless all sections of the Liberian nation, people, friends of Liberia, and the Great "UNITED NATIONS" halt this development. To this end, the Liberian people shall assemble consistently bearing in mind that the Liberian people are the most vital and potent forces to direct changes and developments in their country in peace and that their "Unity" is essential. In view whereof, this conference resolves that peace and democracy be restored in the Republic of Liberia and seriously condemn warfare. This conference, therefore, calls upon the Liberian people to attend as an all-in organization or individual conference of Liberian people in the United States of America whose sure purpose will be to:

1.   Demand the calling of a national "PEACE CONFERENCE" in the city of Monrovia representing all the people of Liberia wherein the fundamental rights of the people will be considered to consolidate the unity of the Liberian people. That to achieve the above, a continuation committee be appointed which will make arrangements for an immediate all-Liberian organization conference to be held by not later than the 16 and 17 of June 1995. This conference is gearing up for the democratic peace restoration in Liberia and demands that:

a.   all warlord factions immediately withdraw their power, arms and ammunition forthwith, and stop the butcherings and let pass persecutions democratically so that an atmosphere can be created for action to be taken to redress the justifiable grievances of the

people whose very existence was admitted by the West African
Peace-Keeping Force commissioned a few years ago. The conference
hails the struggle of the Liberian people who have, by their courage
and determination, exposed the hypocrisy which suggested that
"REBEL" activities are acceptable to the Liberian people both in
the urban and rural areas.

This conference calls upon the Liberian people and Democrats
throughout the world to regard the Liberian's resistance to warfare as an
integral part of the fight against inhumane attitudes.

That this conference will suggest to the "UNITED NATIONS" to send
a team of military peace-keeping force observers to Liberia and to use its
good offices to curb the fight against alarming military operations against
unarmed, disabled people, mostly women and children, which constitute a
threat to peace and democracy in Liberia.

This conference of the Liberian people shall welcome the resolution
of the Security Council of the United Nations and, in particular, the visit
of the Secretary-General, but urges that the Liberian public, through this
organization, "THE VOICE OF LIBERIA" be contacted, in order to have
a true purview of the situation in the country (Liberia).

This conference will wish to place on record that the continual breaking
of the "PEACE" proposal, agreements, by the warlord factions and their
perpetual massacre in the nation (Liberia) and demoralizing to which extent
peace and democracy are denied, are clear indications of their military
leadership plans.

This conference shall demand the immediate halting of all rebel
activities and the evacuation of arms from the soil of Liberia without further
consideration. By all means, continual intimidation and humiliation of our
poor, innocent, needy, disarmed people of Liberia must immediately stop.

The senseless continual building of so-called checkpoints in all parts of
Liberia for the purpose of harassment, molestation, dehumanization and
intimidation must be eradicated. The leadership of Liberia must be achieved
through democratic process, (free and fair general elections), not by arms.

The operations of foreign investors in Liberia be halted until a genuine
civilian government takes control of the land. It has been observed and
noted that some of the warlord factions are using the mineral resources of
the land to purchase arms.

The Ambassadors of the following African countries shall be contacted
by this August Body: the Republic of Ivory Coast, the Republic of Guinea,

the Republic of Sierra Leone, Libya, and the Republic of Burkina-Faso and informed of the organization's position and concern.

Supporters of the warlord faction leaders shall be discouraged and seriously warned against same. Cargoes leaving Liberia to any country for any purpose whatsoever, be embargoed and returned or restored for safe-keeping under international law until further notice from the United Nations authorities or the like. All financial aid packages for Liberia shall be halted until "Peace and true Democracy" is restored through electoral process. Any interim government that is in power now or one that will be instituted in the country should embrace the involvement of a representative of the United Voice of Liberia in the United States.

Liberia was founded on Christian principles:

No particular ethnic group should or shall be encouraged to suppress, oppress, or massacre another ethnic group in the Republic rampantly. Anybody who had, at one time, deployed foreign military power into Liberia for the sure purpose of raging war on the nation or causing severe damage in the nation will not be or should not be permitted to run for a leadership position of any kind.

Aspiring candidates must be examined by the Liberian public in the country and abroad. Any aspiring candidate, contesting on the basis of tribalism, sectionalism, academic arrogance, or the like should be disqualified. Based upon the nation's past and present experiences with "COUP" leading to civil/tribal war, anybody or a group who assassinates a president should be charged with murder. No soldier or soldiers shall be allowed to leave his or her or their military barracks with fire-arms or silent weapons, except in an extreme emergency under the control of a specific command for a very limited period of time as the law of the land may prescribe.

All checkpoints leading into Liberia should be guarded by police, immigration, and custom officials only, not armed soldiers. This organization, the UNITED VOICE of LIBERIA, should remain consistently calm and follow a policy of non-violence. It should conduct itself peaceably at all times, regardless of direct or indirect attacks from anybody of authority. It will do so because the members prefer peaceful methods of change to achieve their aspirations without the suffering and bitterness of civil war again, as it has been in the past.

But the people's "PATIENCE" is not immortal.

The time comes in the life of anybody or a group when there remains only two alternatives; submit or cry louder. This time is now in the Liberian situation. We shall not be quiet and we have no choice but to speak out by all means within our power in defense of our people, our future and our peace and democratic restoration.

In these actions, we are working in the best interests of all the people of this nation of Liberia—Gio, Mano, Kpelle, Gola, Mandingo, Bassa, Kru, Krahn, Grebo, Lorma, Via, and all tribes and residents whose fustaff and the caretaker of a patient were treated for injuries. Most of the patients who could walk fled the hospital; many others were taken away by their family members.

This was the second time that planes attacked, the first being on November 5, 1992, although no buildings were hit. In October 1992, when the ECOMOG air attacks began, the International Committee of the Red Cross had helped the staff of Phebe Hospital to paint large red crosses on the roof to avoid accidental attack.

According to reports in *The Independent* and *The Washington Post*, the bombing raid on Greenville March 18 lasted 25 minutes and killed at least 15 civilians, although the exact numbers are difficult to compile since most of the population fled after the attack. The F. J. Grante Hospital was also hit, causing all the doctors, nurses and patients to flee.

On April 18, an MSF convoy carrying medicines and vaccines was attacked after leaving the Ivory Coast by four ECOMOG jets just outside the town of Sanniquelle in Nimba County. The convoy was clearly marked with the organization's insignia. An MSF spokesperson said the attack had forced the organization to suspend cross-border operations from the Ivory Coast. "This violent attack against a clearly identified relief convoy marks a serious escalation in the threats against humanitarian operations in the country," according to MSF.

Africa Watch calls upon ECOMOG to conduct a thorough investigation into the targets of its air raids. In addition, explicit guarantees should be provided for the neutrality of hospitals and humanitarian relief operations.

The Armed Forces of Liberia (AFL)

The AFL wants to be viewed as the legitimate government army, not just a warring faction. In fact, their status is unclear; in many respects, the AFL is regarded as the army of the Interim Government, as illustrated by the fact that IGNU's minister of defense is ostensibly in charge of the AFL. IGNU occasionally makes statements referring to the AFL as their nominal army, and IGNU has paid honorariums to AFL. As the AFL Chief of Staff put it,

"AFL is a party to the conflict, but it is proving itself to be a national army, not like in 1990." This statement clearly indicates that the AFL did not understand the clear implication of being classified as the national army of Liberia. Accordingly, AFL should have taken control of the Executive Mansion following the death of its chief Doe in September, 1990; then called on the international community for military aid. In any case, they should never be considered as a faction or part of the conflict as their chief of staff said. Because they have failed and disappointed the Liberian public. It is a great shame for them to consider themselves as part to the conflict. The AFL ought to have been the host for ECOMOG in Liberia, if AFL ever really knew and understood its position.

However, as a party to the conflict according to them, its behavior during 1990 was as reprehensible as any of the other factions simply because they did not know their position as a national army. Since Prince Johnson killed Samuel K. Doe and then refused to enter the Executive Mansion, that was a chance left for AFL to take-over and call for international aid effective immediately.

I believe that their understanding was that it was only Doe whom they were there to protect, not the Constitution nor the Executive Mansion of the country from invading forces. This is very wrong, wrong and wrong. I hope the national army will in the future learn from this mistake and correct it.

However, I salute them for being so calm. From the November 1990 cease-fire until it was attacked on October 15, the AFL was effectively encamped and maintained a fairly low profile. All that has changed since October, and AFL is back on the scene. A pattern has now emerged of AFL soldiers engaging in looting and armed robbery, with the civilian population fearing reprisals if they report the incidents. The danger posed by the renewed AFL presence in the city was described by a Liberian journalist; "The AFL loses direction. They become drunk with material things. They just want to loot. If someone gets in their way, they charge him with being a rebel and kill him."

To most Liberians, the AFL is virtually synonymous with looting. On January 26, 1993, when the AFL arrived at the Exchem plant near Robertsfield, one of the Liberian workers there described the AFL conduct as follows: "The AFL came in and we came out—with our hands up. We were unarmed and identified ourselves. Before they took us to their headquarters, they looted all 10 houses in the compound. They took videos, furniture, clothing, jewelry, dishes, pots—every imaginable thing in ten houses. There were forty to fifty AFL soldiers . . . ECOMOG is allowing the AFL to commit too many atrocities. They are going around with such vengeance. Look at us, all civilians, no soldiers. They looted everything. ECOMOG said nothing about the confiscated property."

Another fellow standing with hands on his head said to his wife, "I think all African soldiers are criminals and only out there to loot in time of trouble." His wife replied, "Don't think white men will do this to us either; especially American soldiers, in time of distress." On one occasion, I had the opportunity to interview an old soldier who was victimized in the situation. This is what he said, "My son, black man is just black man, he can come from under the ground or up in the sky; he has his black heart. ECOMOG or whoever, they call them, I don't trust a bit of them; because I know they will never help their brothers. Rather they will make their burden heavier. I do not know why the white people did not come. Well, we will look to God."

During my many interviews with the civilian population, all linked to the United States for trust, honesty, sincerity and dependibility for their lives; not any force from within Africa. Today, if one interviews any civilian in Liberia, concerning the numerous peace agreements made and failed, she or he will definitely tell you that it is so, because the Americans have not yet been involved in the entire process.

One of the workers at the Liberian Blood Research Center near Robertsfield went back to the Lab in early 1993 to feed and clean the Chimpanzees and saw AFL soldiers engaged in extensive looting.

However, the looting attitude of AFL did not just start today. This started when we were yet unborn. The main reason(s) behind this persistent looting is that these soldiers were never paid. Some would hardly get food for their family nor money to pay children's school fees. This treatment on the part of a national government encourages dishonesty among its citizens in employment at all levels.

I am a victim of this act. In 1985, when the Doe regime accused Mr. William Gabriel Kpoleh of helping somebody to overthrow Doe's government, I was then chairperson for the political party—LUP. Since Mr. Kpoleh was its national standard bearer, I was forced out of my house by soldiers and it was also looted. After which one of the soldiers explained to me that "Our commander told us whatever we see take it as our pay."

Is this how a national government should pay its soldiers? In the future Liberia needs to take good care of its national guards better than this. The national security of any government will only be honest, sincere and dedicated when the government can ably handle its staff needs properly and adequately.

According to my observation, Charles G. Taylor seems to possess these genuine characteristics of a good leader: sharing, concern, protection and defense. But as human behavior gets involved, he was misundertood in the late Doe's administration. He ordered vehicles for all those who were working for government up to the President himself when he was Director of GSA. Others would have never done this sort of thing; rather they would have only pocketed the sum.

During the civil crisis of 1990 to the time I left, he was very much concerned about his common people as he always said. He often demonstrates good leadership abilities in his territory. But let's not forget that during war time or in situations as this, every individual has his or her personal agenda only; thereby making it very difficult to control the people. Before the crisis there were a lot of problems in existence among the ethnic groups in Nimba County.

I strongly want to believe that if this man was not interrupted by people of political ambitions, there should have never been any civil unrest in Liberia. But as a human being, he felt hurt when the very people who today claim to be leaders in Doe's regime fled and escaped, leaving the poor people in the hot-fire of Doe's regime. These people didn't think of their people while in the United States until Doe was assassinated in 1990. In this light, I suppose we should treat this matter with fairness.

We may also understand that every country that has been involved in civil crisis as this, also faced numerous problems as those Liberians are now facing throughout the world. We need absolute unity and respect for each other. It is now time for positive thinking for all peace-loving Liberians in Liberia and outside. I salute all Liberians who have learned and are still learning; it is through this medium that we shall be able to build a genuine and valuable nation for all. Therefore, we need to conduct and demonstrate positive attitudes towards each other in all walks of life in Liberia and abroad.

Liberia is at the cross-road of life and death; as the speaker once said, we must choose life with dignity, sincerity, honesty, love and concern. Lies, bearing false witness, rumors without foundation, hatred and wicked jealousy cannot build a modern, civilized nation.

It is my personal view that many baseless accusations have been leveled against one another by people in Monrovia and its environs during this civil war; which perhaps can never be proven. To those against whom these accusations have been pronounced during a time of conflict such as this, people often go against each other falsely. I, therefore, admonish you to be patient and understanding in all your dealings. I pray that you do not hold these things against your accusers forever.

Liberians have always been Christians and understanding people; however, as humans err, sometimes, they crash. Remember that too many people are totally confused and frustrated by the atrocities which they might have never expected. For one hundred forty-two years of the nation's independence, we have never experienced this sort of thing.

Let me mention another area of concern. It involves the nation's national army's (AFL) ability to arrest and detain civilians, often on dubious grounds. The AFL contends that it only imprisons people for looting, armed robbery and suspicion of rebel activity. However, there are also cases of people being arrested on charges of "impersonating the AFL," which means that he was wearing an AFL uniform. Africa Watch interviewed detainees at the Post Stockade, the infamous AFL prison at the Barclay Training Center (BTC) in Monrovia, who had been arrested for driving AFL soldiers to pick up their looted goods in Harbel. They assert that because they owned vehicles, they were approached by AFL soldiers to drive them to Harbel and back. The soldiers told them to wear an AFL jacket so as to avoid suspicion at checkpoints. On their return to Monrovia, the vehicles were stopped at a checkpoint and only the drivers were arrested; the soldiers went free with their loot. The drivers have since been released without the due process of law.

You can clearly see that people are perhaps confused and do not observe the constitution any longer in their daily activities. Many are accused and released on a daily basis without court trial.

Court Martials

In October, the AFL set up a court martial board, based on the Uniform Code of Military Justice (UCM). Although the AFL should be encouraged to investigate and try its own soldiers, the court martial boards must operate with full guarantees of due process and not resort to scapegoating. However, some of these trials seem to fall into the latter category.

The first trial involved Private Tarawally Mannie, accused and found guilty of murdering Mohammed Kenneth in late October. Though Mannie pleaded not guilty, on November 21, the AFL publicly executed him. General Hezekiah Bowen, chief of staff of the AFL, announced that the execution was an example of what would happen to soldiers caught looting and killing.

Mannie's trial lacked any semblance of due process; he was not provided with competent counsel, and no appeal was requested. He was sentenced on November 20 and executed the next day, even though, the trial record was supposed to be reviewed by a judge advocate. There was no time for any review or for the president to sign the execution warrant, as required by the Liberian code of Law.

Mannie told foreign journalists he was being set up. He claimed that it was dark when the incident took place, and admits seeing two people and shooting at them. He then took the injured man for medical treatment, where he died a few days later.

The day of his execution, Mannie was blindfolded with a black handkerchief covering his face, and was paraded around the Barclay Training Center (the AFL barracks in Monrovia) in a pick-up truck. With great fanfare, he was then taken to South Beach, outside the AFL barracks, and executed in front of a large crowd. It is worth noting that the execution took place on the same beach where, after the 1980 coup, then Master Sergeant Samuel K. Doe executed 13 ministers from the government of President William R. Tolbert Jr.

One Liberian journalist who witnessed the execution described it as follows:

It was medieval. The guy was dead before the first bullet, while he was being paraded around. It was too nasty. His father had warned him not to join the army, that it was a tribal business. He was a Grebo; the next one executed was a Kpelle guy.

The next case brought before the Court Martial Board involved an AFL soldier, Papa Say. On November 23 he was charged with murder under Art. 118 of the UCMJ for killing a civilian, Siapha Gray, on November 14 in Monrovia. The trial lasted from December 3-18, and he was found guilty. Say was executed on December 28. This time President Sawyer signed the execution warrant.

On December 16, 1992, two other AFL soldiers, First Sergeant Isaac Caine and Private Sampson Tarley, were charged with murder under Art. 118 of the UCMJ. They were accused of murdering Private Solo Quarty on November 16. The charges against Tarley were dropped and Caine was acquitted in February 1993.

The Murder of Brian Gamham

In one high profile case in January 1993, Brian Gamham, a British citizen working at the Liberian Institute for Biomedical Research, an affiliate of the New York Blood Center, was killed by the AFL. The lab is located near Robertsfield, which had been controlled by the NPFL since 1990.

They conducted medical research on hepatitis and river blindness using chimpanzees and there were 120 chimpanzees at the lab.

Gamham and his American wife, Betsy Brotman, had lived in Liberia for many years. Since the NPFL had taken control of Robertsfield, they had their share of problems with the young fighters, but managed to get along with the NPFL. As Brotman put it, "In a situation like that, you have to get along with everyone. They (the NPFL) were cordial, but not intimate. Individual soldiers harassed us—they wanted gas, or cars—and they were often unpleasant at checkpoints."

Nevertheless, when the ECOMOG bombings began in their area in November 1992, Gamham and Brotman became openly critical of ECOMOG. In December 1992, they tried to write to the United Nations envoy, Trevor Gordon-Sommers (see below, The United Nations), to inform him about the bombing of Harbel. The letter was never sent, but was leaked to the BBC and broadcast.

Throughout the civil war, we have had the cooperation of the NPRA government. They have given us every assistance during 1990-91 when we were feeding over 27,000 refugees and had five supplementary feeding programs. It is our belief that the Monrovian government headed by Amos Sawyer has now become the Nigeria/ECOMOG puppet government. It is our belief that ULIMO and the former Doe forces (AFL) have been aided and abetted by ECOMOG. ECOMOG can no longer be considered a non-biased, peacekeeping force.

In mid-January, as the fighting approached Robertsfield, ECOMOG was notified of the presence of civilians at the laboratory. According to Patricia Gullert, the Director of Veterinary Services at the Lab, ECOMOG was informed in several ways—Betsy Brotman, Gamham's wife, sent telexes from the lab; Fred Prince, the lab's founder and the director of the New York Blood Center, contaced the U.S. State Department; and Gullet herself went to the Nigeria Embassy in Abidjan and the U.S. Embassy in Monrovia, which in turn spoke to the ECOMOG command. Gullet explained:

We were assured that ECOMOG understood where we were, that we were noncombatants and not to be molested. So we felt fairly secur that nothing would happen. Later, when Betsy and I went to talk to General Olurin, he was furious. "We knew you were there. I myself told ULIMO and AFL that you were not to be molested. I said white people were not to be molested. I did that to cover you." He was very angry. But he should have known better. They let the AFL go first, and then let them loot, then leave and then ECOMOG calls it a secure area.

Witnesses report that on Sunday, January 31, the AFL arrived at the compound. There were still a number of people in the compound, those who worked at the lab as well as other civilians who were trapped there by the fighting. About 25-30 of them gathered downstairs in the house farthest from the gate and nearest to the lab. Brotman went upstairs, and Gamham followed her. Three soldiers wearing green uniforms with AFL patches on their arms kicked down the door. As Brotman later told Africa Watch:

"Brian must have seen something in their eyes, because he seemed to know what was happening. He dropped to his knees and said, 'My son, I beg you, don't—and then he was shot'." They didn't give him a chance; he was a dead man. They shot him in the abdomen. They ripped off my chain, took my watch. The one who killed Brian started looting.

After the killing, AFL soldiers went on a looting spree, emptying the laboratory compound of whatever they could carry. A few hours later all those in the compound had been taken to her husband's body. "By that time," she said, "All the animals—our pets—were dead. The house was looted; the computer was gone, all the audio stuff was gone. The place was loaded up because they were storing things for the ones who had already left."

The investigation launched by IGNU into Gamham's death does not inspire much confidence that the perpetrators will be identified and punished. A commission of inquiry was formed which met at IGNU's Ministry of Defense, headed by AFL General Pelham, and included representatives of the AFL and IGNU's Ministry of Justice.

Although outside observers were invited to participate in the inquiry, including the Catholic Church's Justice and Peace Commission and the U.S. Embassy, they have been excluded from important meetings on security grounds. In March, the Justice and Peace Commission pulled out. By all accounts, the commission was reluctant to blame the AFL, which is trying to recast its image as the legitimate national army. Reports indicate that as of late April, the only witness who had been interviewed was Gamham's wife, Betsy Brotman, and that at her initiative. Interviews with officials of both the NPFL and ECOMOG reveal a transparent effort to absolve the killers. These officials claim that since Gamham and Brotman held NPFL identity cards which stated "the holder of this card must not in any way be molested or disarmed," Gamham must have been armed and a member of the NPFL, even though that is not grounds for murder. They refuse to concede that many civilians working in NPFL territory were given such ID cards in 1990, without which they would have suffered harassment by NPFL fighters.

The commission is also apparently relying on exculpatory statements from the AFL front-line commanders, even though all evidence suggests that it was the AFL that executed him.

On February 5, ECOMOG issued a statement condemning the killing and calling on the AFL to conduct a full investigation.

In early April, the Ministry of Defense decided to replace the chair of the commission, General Pelham, with General William Dennis, who had served as co-chair under Pelham. The change was reportedly due to dissatisfaction within IGNU concerning the lack of progress in the investigation.

The last week of April, five AFL soldiers, including two officers, were charged in connection with Gamham's murder; however none was charged with murder. The most severe charges were brought against the platoon commander, Captain Gbazai Gaye, who was charged under Art. 131 of the UCMJ for perjury, and under Art. 134 of the UCMJ, a general article covering disorders and neglect of the discipline of the armed forces.

The Ulimo Factor

The United Liberation Movement for Democracy in Liberia (ULIMO) was formed in 1991 by former AFL soldiers who had fled to Sierra Leone. The formal connections between the AFL and ULIMO are difficult to verify, although at least 10 of ULIMO's political key commanders are former AFL officers, including the field commander, General Joe November Harris. ULIMO's political agenda is unclear, despite its claim to seek peace and democracy for the country. It was ULIMO's incursion in August 1992 that set the stage for the renewed war.

Taylor immediatelly charged that ULIMO was in cahoots with ECOMOG. This view was shared by many other observers. As one foreign relief worker put it:

> "Their (ULIMO's) sudden logistical capacity to clear the NPFL
> out of those areas in a couple of weeks made it extremely hard to
> believe otherwise."

Human rights language is notably absent from his report, which was released in mid-March, thus missing yet another occasion to insert human rights protections into the peace negotiations. His report attempts to explain the Liberian conflict without antagonizing the parties to the conflict. Regarding the ECOMOG air raids, for example, the report only noted that, "Mr. Taylor complained that persistent bombing attacks by ECOMOG of civilian targets, as recently as 27 February 1993, resulted in extensive casualties."

The report suggested that there might be a role for U.N. observers, approximately 200, to monitor a new cease-fire agreement, but foresaw no human rights monitoring component to their mandate. This is an unfortunate omission, since it would have afforded an unprecedented opportunity for transparency throughout the country.

In an effort to address Taylor's refusal to disarm to ECOMOG in its current composition, the U.N. suggests broadening ECOMOG to include other ECOWAS members while retaining the present command structure.

The need to involve broader elements of civil society—especially elders, community leaders and women's groups—in the process of a reconciliation conference, organized and conducted by Liberians, which would address particular participatory democracy, the strengthening of civil society and reconstruction and development of the country. This is a critical point which deserves greater emphasis; the encouragement and strengthening of civil society throughout the country must be a priority. Already in Monrovia, there are significant aspects of civil society that are functioning. These include a lively, independent press, with newspapers such as *The Inquirer, The Eye and The Daily News*; at least four independent human rights organizations—The Catholic Peace and Justice Commission, The Center for Law and Human Rights Education, the Liberian Human Rights Chapter and the Association of Human Rights Promoters; relief groups, such as Self; medical groups, such as Mercy and the Christian Health Association of Liberia (CHAL); university-related organizations; children's protection groups, such as the Children's Assistance Program (CAP) and Liberian Children's Concern (LICHCCO), and church groups.

When the prospects for long-term rehabilitation of Liberian society are contemplated, few ingredients will be as critical as the status of civil society. Meanwhile the question of civil society in territory occupied by the NPFL and ULIMO has to be addressed, and efforts made to nurture independent initiatives that are attempting to function.

On March 26, the Security Council unanimously passed resolution 813 on Liberia, which condemned continuing armed attacks against the peacekeeping forces of ECOMOG by one of the parties to the conflict and called upon all warring parties to respect strictly the provisions of international humanitarian law. The resolution makes no mention of ECOMOG's alliance with the other warring factions, or notes any concerns about ECOMOG's conduct of the war, such as the air strikes.

The U.N.'s support of ECOMOG is also linked to financial considerations. The cost of a U.N. peacekeeping operation far exceeds the cost of ECOMOG; the U.N. pays its peacekeeping soldiers almost $1,000 per month, whereas ECOMOG pays its soldiers between $5.00 and $10.00 per day. Another difference is that the U.N. pays the per diems directly to the soldiers' governments, whereas ECOMOG pays the soldiers directly, since the governments are financing their own contingents. As of early 1993, the cost of the entire ECOMOG operation has been approximately $500 million. (Since the U.S. pays some 30% [thirty percent] of U.N. peacekeeping operations, the Clinton Administration has little incentive to draw the U.N. into further involvement in Liberia).

The United States

In 1992 and 1993, the U.S. government continued its policy of not recognizing any government in Liberia—neither the Interim Government nor the National Patriot Front of Liberia (NPFL) operation body, the National Patriotic Reconstruction Assembly. The U.S. also remained publicly committed to supporting ECOWAS and its peace plan.

In addition to humanitarian assistance, the U.S. has provided a total of $8.6 million to ECOWAS for peacekeeping, and $18.75 million in Foreign Military Financing (FMF) and Department of Defense Draw-down (DOD) authority to ECOWAS member states to support ECOMOG. In FY 94, the Clinton Administration has requested $12 million for ECOWAS peacekeeping activities.

The U.S. policy of supporting ECOMOG lost some credibility after the BBC broadcast remarks made by Herman Cohen, then Assistant Secretary of State for African Affairs, on November 11. After an off-the-record briefing given at Harvard University on November 4, Cohen was taped as saying, "ECOWAS is unfortunately no longer a neutral party . . . They are now one of the combatants. I think the next step—and we are discussing this in Washington—will be U.N. intervention to provide a neutral party to try and bring about a political solution."

Cohen tried to clarify his position the following day, when he told the BBC, "I think it must have been a slip of the tongue . . . We have not changed our policy. We still believe in what the West African countries are trying to do, which is to bring about a non-violent democratic solution to Liberia."

In an unusual post-session hearing held by the House Subcommittee on Africa on November 19, Deputy Assistant Secretary of State Leonard

Robinson declared strong U.S. support for ECOMOG; he refused to ciriticize the conduct of their bombing raids, saying only that the U.S. has expressed its concern about civilian casualties and "ECOMOG has assured us that such collateral damage is unintentional." In conclusion, Robinson warned that, "No one who comes to power in Liberia through force or fraud can expect normal relations with the United States."

The same day at the United Nations, U.S. Ambassador Edward Perkins sent a strong signal of support to ECOMOG, but made no mention of the need to protect human rights as part of the peace process.

It is imperative that the regional peacekeeping effort in Liberia succeed. Abandonment of the regional peace process could lead to resumption of warfare and probable humanitarian catastrophe. A bloody take-out by force would deal a set-back to democratic aspirations throughout Africa and lead to the conclusion that might makes right. If the united ECOWAS effort fails in Liberia, the organization is unlikely to venture into the difficult realm of peacekeeping and conflict resolution in the future, and pressure will build rapidly for direct U.S. or U.N. intervention. We owe ECOWAS our full support as they consider means of pressurizing the Liberian warring factions to implement the peace plan calling for disarmament, encampment and free and fair elections.

In November 1992, a series of U.S. government cables were leaked to the NPFL, which in turn released them to the press. The cables appear to be authentic, and provide revealing insights into the U.S. attitude toward ECOMOG, as well as the strained relations between the Senegalese and Nigerian contingents.

One cable from October 1992 indicated that the U.S. was well aware of the allegations of ECOMOG bombings of civilian targets, and noted that the peacekeepers risked losing international support. The cable also reveals that the Senegalese had unofficially informed the U.S. that they intended to withdraw from ECOMOG because they are "tired of their heavy role in bolstering ECOMOG's combat capability." The cable notes that such a withdrawal would "cripple ECOMOG." Another cable from the U.S. embassy stated:

> "ECOMOG, since the 15th, has not acquitted itself with distinction, with the notable exception of the Senegalese and Guineans. Some elements of the other contingents have been worse than useless, repeatedly abandoning positions without a fight and leaving to others the task of recovering terrain. One glaring area of difference between the contending groups is that, we think, Taylor

has superb intelligence on ECOMOG and IGNU, while those two
know much less about Taylor's capabilities and intentions."

Regarding AFL and ULIMO, the cable goes on to state that they are
"still constituted primarily of Krahn and Mandingos, who are polarized
potential vengeance seekers. Both, also, are ill-disciplined and disorganized,
and the re-appearance of weapons provides means to revert to thuggery as
well as more serious score-settling."

Another cable, dated October 28, made clear that the U.S. had
encouraged the ECOWAS peace process in large part because the U.S. did
not want to get involved in Liberia.

As a result of these leaks, State Department sources have reported that the
ECOMOG commanders are very reluctant to inform the U.S. about their
strategies and internal operations. As of May 1993—six months after the
appearance of the cables—there has been little apparent effort by U.S. officials
to deal with the leak. One State Department official called the situattion
"inexcusable," and noted that it reflected the lack of interest by the U.S.
government in Africa. But I strongly disagree with that sort of assumption.

In an unusual statement critical of the AFL and ULIMO, U.S. Charge d'
Affaires William Twaddell delivered a letter to the independent newspaper,
The Inquirer, apparently in response to an *Inquirer* editorial on March 5 that
denounced the widespread looting by AFL and ULIMO. Twaddell's letter
condemned the "frenzied looting of properties" and went on to state:

"Another disturbing trend along with this rampant trade in stolen goods
is the blossoming in the city streets of armed men in uniforms as they traffic
in their ill-gotten booty. These men, be they members of AFL or ULIMO,
are obviously not engaged in safeguarding the population or otherwise
contributing to the image or reality of Monrovia as a safe haven.

He is to be commended for making this public statement about such a
rampant abuse. However, no similar statement was issued from Washington,
which would carry greater weight. Similarly, the U.S. has refrained from
openly criticizing ECOMOG bombing or the human rights implications
of its alliance with ULIMO and the AFL.

ASSESSMENTS
AND RECOMMENDATIONS

THE U.S. IS CLEARLY AWARE of the increasing human rights problems associated with the ECOMOG intervention, yet U.S. policy still revolves around full support for ECOMOG. There is an obvious discrepancy between what American officials say in private as evidenced by the leaked cables and other statements intended to be off-the-record, and their public positions. Given the Clinton Administration's latest request for $12 million for ECOWAS's peacekeeping activities, the U.S. is likely to have considerable leverage over ECOMOG's behavior. It is critical for the Administration to make clear its concern about human rights violations by both ECOMOG and the forces with which it is allied, and condition its aid on respect for human rights.

The U.S. should apply to Liberia the approach being pursued by the U.S. for the Vienna Conference on Human Rights, described in the draft U.S. Human Rights Action Plan. Under this plan, the U.S. calls for human rights to be "an integrated element of all U.N. peacekeeping, humanitarian, conflict resolution, elections monitoring, development programs, and other activities." It goes on to state that the human rights work should be included in peacekeeping operations, as has been done in El Salvador and Cambodia.

Accountability for Past Abuses

Africa Watch believes that those responsible for egregious human rights abuses in Liberia must be held accountable for their crimes. As we have set forth in our policy statement on accountability for past abuses, it is the responsibility of governments to seek accountability, regardless of whether the perpetrators are officials of the government, the military, anti-government forces, or others.

We also oppose any laws that purport to immunize those who have committed gross abuses from exposure of their crimes to civil suits for damages for those crimes, or from criminal investigation, prosecution and punishment.

One of the tragedies of Liberia is that the issue of accountability has been avoided in all the peace negotiations. There is no mention in any of the Yamoussoukro documents or their follow-up meetings about the issue of accountability.

There is growing discussion of a general amnesty for all combatants. The report of the All Liberia Conference of March-April 1991 resolved that a "conditional amnesty be granted to all Liberians who served as combatants in the civil war of Liberia" but it does not elaborate. Many Liberians also fear that a blanket amnesty would lead to a wave of vengeance killings with individuals settling scores on their own.

Seeking accountability does not contradict these calls for a conditional amnesty. Africa Watch does not oppose an amnesty for the offense of taking up arms for general acts of war, but strongly opposes an amnesty for war crimes or crimes against humanity.

Many Liberians express the fear that any effort to seek accountability for past abuses will destroy the fragile fabric of Liberian society, that too many people have too much blood on their hands. One expatriate with long experience in Liberia put it this way:

"Where do you start? When do you start? At this point, there are so many people involved at various points of time. Maybe you could go after some of the more flagrant ones. There are plenty of names from the AFL—from 1985, from 1990—and you've got the NPFL, the INPFL and now ULIMO. As I said, where do you start? Accountability is unlikely. There are so many people involved that if you start it, everyone's going to be pointing fingers at everyone else."

Africa Watch recognizes the difficulty that some governments may face in holding members of their own armed forces accountable for human rights abuses, but we do not believe that these difficulties justify disregard for the principle of accountability. Despite these obstacles, the alternative is far worse. It is important to note that our position calling for investigation, prosecution and punishment of those responsible for gross abuses is premised on a reconstituted court system that would conform to internationally recognized principles of due process of law.

Until such time as a court system could handle cases of accountability for past abuses, some form of Truth Commission might be established, on the model of El Salvador, to avoid acts of revenge. In El Salvador, a group of distinguished persons were appointed by the U.N.'s Secretary General to conduct a six-month review of grave acts of violence, whose mark on society demands with great urgency public knowledge of the truth. The 1992 peace accord in El Salvador also established the militia's Tubmanburg headquarters last month. "They are prisoners of war and we will keep them until we have finished interrogating them," he said.

He said five ULIMO loyalists, most of whom are from Kromah's Mandingo tribe, were taken prisoners when they sought refuge in an ECOMOG camp during the fighting but he did not make the Nigerians' release conditional on the freeing of his men.

He said the dissidents lost four hundred men during the battle forty miles (64km) northwest of the capital city of Monrovia, but his own forces suffered only (10-15) dead.

He explained the disparity in casualties by saying that most of the Krahn fighters joined ULIMO from the Armed Forces of Liberia (AFL), the former national army that collapsed into a tribal militia after the December 1989 outbreak of civil war and the killing the next year of Krahn President Samuel Doe.

"They are conventional soldiers, my boys are guerrillas, bush fighers, they hit the enemy before he sees them coming," he said.

Kromah said his men also enjoyed the advantage of magic charms that rendered them invulnerable.

"About 35 to 40 percent of my men are bullet-proof, and not from vests," he said. Fighting was still going on in the Tubmanburg region and his men were advancing on Krahn holding the Po River bridge, which commands the road into ULIMO territory from Monrovia, Kromah continued.

Kromah said he was in Guinea, which contributes troops to ECOMOG, to brief President Lansana Conte on developments in Liberia and talk to U.N. relief officials about prospects of shipping food and medicine from Guinea to Liberia's Lofa County, cut off from Monrovia by fighting and poor roads.

Cote d'Ivoire

Abidjan, Ivory Coast, on July 25, 1993, Liberia's civil war protagonists signed a long-awaited peace accord, pledging to start disarming and installing a transitional government within thirty days.

A year later, fewer than 10 percent of an estimated 30,000 fighters have laid down their guns, the government can do little outside the capital of

Monrovia, and the shaky truce between the main players is threatened by a proliferation of warlords.

"It's getting more and more like Somalia every day and a lot of people believe it will become worse than Somalia," a United Nations official told Reuters in neighboring Ivory Coast. "There are flare-ups everywhere. Even the main highways, although they are open, cannot be called safe," she said.

The leaders of the two biggest militias, Charles Taylor and Alhaji Kromah, could probably agree on most issues and find ways to work together, judging by their publicly-stated positions. But both men are kept off-balance by attacks from the Krahn tribe, which analysts believe aims to regain by force the ascendancy it enjoyed under slain President Samuel Doe.

Taylor's National Patriotic Front of Liberia (NPFL) is battling Krahn fighters in the east and center of the country and now faces the additional challenge of an internal schism. NPFL ministers in the power-sharing government are turning against the man who put them there and some diplomats believe they have made a secret pact with Krahn gunmen edging toward Taylor's inland capital at Gbarnga.

"The NPFL is not the problem, but rather its leader, Mr. Charles Taylor, who has led the organization astray and continues to dwell on armed struggle . . . because he knows that he cannot win elections," Labor Minister Tom Woewiyu told a Monrovia news conference on Tuesday.

Taylor, who launched the civil war in December 1989, says he is for elections and analysts say he could well draw more votes than any other candidate now on the scene.

Kromah's ULIMO militia also has a Krahn problem. Last May Krahn renegades under General Roosevelt Johnson seized ULIMO headquarters northwest of Monrovia and hundreds of militia men have died in fighting, which is still raging.

Elections, originally scheduled for last February, then September, now appear to be a distant dream. Large parts of the country are still battlegrounds and half of Liberia's two million citizens are refugees in neighboring states.

Even the United Nations, which adhered to the September schedule after others said it was unworkable, now says polling depends on the success of a disarmament drive that has yet seriously to begin.

"Until the disarmament process is substantially accomplished, the holding of free and fair elections will not be possible," a Security Council statement said last week.

The statement told the warring factions to meet by the end of this month and set a target date for disarmament. Foreign electoral advisers say the talks should include the Liberian Peace Council (LPC), a Krahn militia that surfaced after last July's Accord and demands government portfolios.

Taylor opposes participation of the LPC, the group harrying him in the south and east, saying its aggression should not be rewarded. A United Nations official, however, saw no alternative. "They will have to include them if it is to be successful, even though there will be a lot of resentment," she said.

Ivorian officials, alarmed by border incursions and the presence of some 300,000 Liberian refugees on their soil, hope fresh initiatives to resolve the conflict can be agreed at a West African summit due to be held in Nigeria next week.

Liberian leader David Kpomakpor held pre-summit talks with the presidents of neighboring Guinea and Sierra Leone on Wednesday but announced no breakthrough.

Loss and Human Connection

I am going to introduce, explain and discuss briefly the ending through death, desertion or geographical separation; for e.g. of a relationship defined by an actor as "significant or meaningful" this is generally conceived of as a "loss" experience. In this chapter, we will wish to pursue the question; what is lost then? What likens them to each other, and above all, what is the true nature of the social bond?

Attachment, grief, and loss—universally human beings are social animals. This simple statement simplifies the entire multitude of questions. As we lift it up and we see such matters as follows: that the human animal is slow to mature and thus stands in a relationship of need to older members of the species for a considerable period of time; that human behavior is seriously needed in Liberia at this period in time because the human connection in Liberia has already been torn apart since 1980. We can never connect one another with fire-arms, hatred, tribalism intimidation and wicked envy and jealousy.

Today, Liberians are fighting wars in the family, the churches, schools and everywhere in the world. I am disappointed about the situation which exists in the Liberian community in the great United States of America. In that I have also observed and found more fighting among Liberians in the U.S. than inside Liberia itself.

Why do I say this? It is an established fact that we come to this land to learn how to take better care or improve on the care-taking of our old, young, and disabled ones—to run our own peaceful government upon our return; to show concern and care for each other while we are here; that one day when we shall have returned to our own land of nativity, we will show the goodness and brightness of civilized and modernized light to those who were unable to come.

On the contrary, we are going to show them the darkest side of an uncivilized and unmodernized way of life.

HUMAN RIGHTS ABUSES BY THE LIBERIAN PEACE COUNCIL AND THE NEED FOR INTERNATIONAL OVERSIGHT

IN LATE 1993, a new armed faction emerged in Liberia, known as the Liberian Peace Council (LPC), which has been fighting Charles Taylor's National Patriotic Front of Liberia (NPFL) in the southeast of the country. While both sides have been responsible for severe human fights and abuses against the civilian population, in recent weeks the LPC appears to have stepped up its campaign against civilians, especially those it considers to have supported the NPFL. Some 40,000 civilians have been displaced by the fighting, and they describe systematic and gratuitous abuses by LPC.

There are consistent reports that elements of the Nigerian contingent of ECOMOG, the West African peacekeeping force—not the Ghanians or the Ugandians, who are also stationed in the area—are aiding the LPC. Displaced persons and other observers report that the Nigerians are supplying arms and ammunition to the LPC as a way to weaken the NPFL, while profiteering on the side. It is not clear how high up the collaboration goes in the Nigerian contingent.

The United Nations in Liberia, UNOMIL, has a mandate to report on violations of the cease-fire and violations of humanitarian law, but it has not been reporting publicly about the situation in the southeast. By avoiding the human rights issues, UNOMIL is failing to implement its mandate in Liberia.

In April, the U.N. Security Council extended UNOMIL's mandate for another six months, with the provision that the situation be reviewed on May 18. Human Rights Watch/Africa calls on the U.N. to ensure that UNOMIL implements its mandate in Liberia, including the requirement to report on violations of humanitarian law. Human Rights Watch/Africa further calls on ECOMOG to launch an immediate investigation of the charges that members of the Nigerian contingent may be assisting the LPC and making its findings public. profound distrust among the warring factions remain obstacles to lasting peace.

ECOMOG has not sought adequately to control the abusive behavior of the forces with which it is normally allied, or to investigate cases of human rights abuses committed by these forces, including killings, beatings, systematic looting and harassment of civilians.

There have been many reports about ECOMOG involvement in looting and occasional harassment or detention of civilians; although ECOMOG has not been responsible for systematic human rights abuses in the territory it controls. However, there is serious concern about the civilian toll and violations of medical neutrality by ECOMOG's air strikes in NPFL territory. There is no indication that ECOMOG has conducted investigations into these incidents.

None of the ECOWAS-sponsored peace talks included human rights on the agenda, thus making the West African countries complicit in the absence of any discussion of human rights protections or accountability for past abuses.

Since issues of accountability for past abuses was never raised by ECOMOG, ECOWAS or the United Nations, those responsible for gross human rights abuses on all sides of the conflict continue to operate with impunity.

The ECOMOG intervention can be separated into three phases; from August to November 1990, the initial intervention that led to a cease-fire; from November 1990 to October 1992, the fragile truce; and from October 1992 to the present, the renewed war.

Having failed to enforce a peaceful solution to the crisis, ECOMOG has been dragged back into the war, and is considered by many to constitute a warring faction. Its role has changed from peacekeeping to peace enforcing, and its rules of engagement now are more aggressive—they not only can use force if they feel threatened and are empowered to disarm the warring factions, but they can also attack targets that might contribute to a threat against them.

According to ECOMOG Field Commander Maj. General Adelunji Olurin, a peacekeeping force is supposed to act as an impartial arbiter. However, he explained that they were compelled to change their role into peace enforcement.

"If a faction decides to take us on and challenge the peacekeepers, then the enforcement role comes in. We must make all factions comply with the wisdom of others—ECOWAS, the O.A.U., or the U.N. One faction cannot be an obstacle to peace. Then, we will return to our peacekeeping posture."

This new role is substantially different from that of a peacekeeper, since it involves aggressive, military operations directed against only one of the parties to the conflict. ECOMOG's actions raise serious questions about the role of a peacekeeping force, and whether its offensive will preclude it from returning to its prior peacekeeping functions.

The only lasting solution to the Liberian crisis will have to be political, based on respect for human rights; the crisis cannot be solved militarily. Since the begining of the conflict, ECOMOG and ECOWAS have avoided inserting human rights into the peace negotiations, ostensibly for fear of derailing the process; peace, therefore, has been separated from human rights. This is underscored by the alliance ECOMOG has formed since October 1992 with two other Liberian factions—ULIMO and the AFL—whose human rights records range from suspect to abysmal. This, in turn, raises questions about ECOMOG's commitment to human rights, and about the role that human rights should play in the peace process.

ECOMOG supporters maintain that human rights forms the foundation of the peace process, and that explicit human rights concerns will be addressed once a peace agreement is in place. The President of the Interim Government, Amos Sawyer, put it this way:

Human rights is imbedded in the peace process; it is the essence of the democratic process . . . But the first step had to be to stop the fighting—to find out what Taylor wanted, to see how to make concessions to get him to stop fighting, and to convince him to bring his claims to the political process. It didn't work, but the basic principle remains disarmament, encampment and elections. Human rights will then fall in line.

There is little reason to believe that human rights guarantees will be integrated into the peace process, at least not at the initiative of ECOWAS. From November 1990 until October 1992, the two years of the fragile truce, the West African leaders and the international community had ample opportunity to raise human rights issues, including protection for the civilian population and accountability for past human rights abuses. Instead, they have created a situation in which the ultimate of impunity which has plagued Liberia for so long is supreme—contempt for human rights. Accordingly, the ECOWAS leaders, with ECOMOG as their instrument, are contributing to the continuing human rights abuses in Liberia.

There is no human rights component to the Yamoussoukro IV accord of October 1991.

The Liberian Peace Council and NPFL

The fighting between Charles Taylor's NPFL and a relatively new faction, calling itself the Liberian Peace Council (LPC), began in October 1993 and continues at this writing. The LPC claims to control six counties—Sinoen Rand, Gedeh, River Cess, Grand Kru, Maryland, and Grand Bassa. The fighting, which began in the area of Grand Kola, got as far as the L.A.C. plantation in early February, and had reached the outskirts of Buchanan by late April.

Little is known about the LPC. The LPC emerged after the Cotonou peace agreement was signed by the NPFL, ULIMO and the interim government in July 1993. It is clear that the LPC is an offshoot of former President Samuel K. Doe's army, the Armed Force of Liberia, and of the Krahn wing of ULIMO. It is composed mainly of people from the Krahn ethnic group. The LPC was formed because the Mandingos (ULIMO) weren't going to spill blood to liberate Grand Gedeh (the county where many of the Krahn live), a well-informed, foreign observer in Monrovia noted. The only way to get the LPC to disarm is to convince ECOMOG that they will be safe with Taylor in the government.

The LPC's strength is estimated to be some 800 fighters, organized into mobile combat units. It is headed by George Boley, a Krahn and former minister of education in the Doe government . . . also formerly a member of ULIMO.

According to Boley, the LPC was formed because of continued acts of atrocities by the NPFL in southeastern Liberia since the Cotonou agreement. He also claimed that most of his fighters were refugees from the Ivory Coast who had been forced to flee from the NPFL. Boley described the LPC as a broad-based national entity which advocates the protection of the rights of exiled and displaced citizens and residents of Liberia as well as the restoration of constitutional democratic leadership in Liberia.

In recent statements, LPC spokespersons have made clear that they will continue fighting until they are included in the transitional government. LPC Secretary General Octavious Walker told reporters on April 14 that the LPC wanted six seats in the transitional parliament as well as portfolios in the interim government, but that discussions with the NPFL had failed to produce an agreement on amending the Cotonou Accord to include the LPC. "We will fight on until they include us in the administrative process," he said.

LPC and NPFL Attacks on Civilians

Thousands of civilians have been displaced by the fighting with some 40,000 registered in the city of Buchanan alone, according to international relief organizations. Testimony from displaced persons and foreign observers indicates that the LPC is responsible for serious human rights abuses against the civilian population, especially those the LPC considers to have supported the NPFL. Abuses include widespread looting, arbitrary arrest and detention, forcible recruitment, beatings, torture, and extrajudicial executions.

The NPFL has also been responsible for abuses against civilians. When the NPFL recaptures a village from the LPC, the inhabitants are often considered to have collaborated with the LPC. In one incident reported in January 1994 in Yapperstown, the NPFL killed eight women and nine men whom they accused of helping the LPC. As a foreign national in Buchanan noted, "It's terminal either way. If the NPFL comes, they say you are LPC, and visa versa."

David, a displaced Bassa man who arrived in Buchanan in late April, described the way civilians have suffered at the hands of both factions. "First the NPFL took our things. They killed my brother's pregnant wife in November 1993. My brother survived and told me about the killing. Then, he said, the LPC came; they told the whole village to leave. We escaped—about 300 or 400 of us—and went to the bush for two months."

In some cases, the displaced persons either do not know, or are afraid to reveal, which faction was responsible for the attack. One very elderly man interviewed by Human Rights Watch/Africa in a Buchanan hospital had been shot in the chest and had his right hand smashed by the same fighter. "It's just gratuitous violence," a foreign relief worker commented.

There are many cases of villages being burned by either the NPFL or the LPC, and sometimes both factions destroyed part of the village at different times. Among the villages in the southeast reportedly burned include the following: Darsaw Town, Debah Town, Johnsoo Town, Bleabeh Town (almost entirely burned by the LPC then the NPFL burned what remained), Jamestown (burned by the NPFL), Talotown (burned by both NPFL and LPC), Tubmanville (burned by LPC), Yapperstown, Flayzor Town.

The majority of the displaced are women, children, and the elderly; able-bodied men are usually arrested and either forcibly recruited or incarcerated. Many of the displaced are suffering from bullet wounds, dehydration, or malnutrition. Some civilians were caught in cross-fire, but others were clearly targeted.

Abuses by the LPC

While both sides are responsible for widespread looting, arbitrary arrests, beatings, and extrajudicial executions, it appears that the LPC has stepped up its campaign against civilians. On one day in mid-April, displaced persons arrived in Buchanan, having been tortured with roasted cutlasses by the LPC. The men were burned on their backs and on their genitals; the women were beaten.

The Following Cases Were Reported to Human Rights Watch/Africa

J., a medical worker from River Cess, fled the fighting with eighteen of his relatives in late February 1994. He was arrested by the LPC on March 3 in Neetown, apparently because he had an identity card issued by the NPFL's civilian arm (the NPRAG) which the LPC took as proof that he fought with the NPFL. His relatives were allowed to continue to Buchanan, but he was subjected to a form of torture known as "tabey." Although one LPC fighter wanted to execute him, another fighter intervened and brought him to the battalion commander, a former AFL colonel. He was then taken to a makeshift jail. Despite their threats, J. refused to state that he was an NPFL rebel.

During his imprisonment, he was forced to work for the fighters performing such functions as picking cassava, cutting wood, digging for copper, and picking coconuts. There were approximately seventy-five other men in the jail with him, all civilians from the Bassa ethnic group. The women, girls, and children were held separately in a church building, and it was believed that many of the women were raped by the LPC.

In earlly April, a young man was identified by an LPC fighter to be a NPFL rebel. Although he denied the charge, the LPC arrested him and tied him up. The fighters roasted their cutlasses in a fire and then burned the man over various parts of his body. Since the man continued to deny the allegation, one of the fighters decided to take more drastic measures to force the confession. He got his army knife and cut out the man's right eye. At that point, the battalion commander arrived, angry because he had not ordered such treatment. However, since they had no means to care for the wounded man, the commander ordered him to be executed. Five LPC fighters took the man into the bush and killed him with cutlasses.

On February 3, 1994, the LPC captured Gorwor Town and began searching the civilians. They found three young men, one about fifteen years old, the other two in their early twenties. When searching the youngest one they found a Charles Taylor T-shirt in his bag. On the back was written "Ghanky" Ok. All three young men were then shot.

Moses, a twenty-seven-year-old medical worker, was arrested by the LPC fighters in Newcess Beach and forced to work as a combat medical personnel. When he tried to refuse, three Krahn soldiers beat him severely almost to death.

Violations of Medical Neutrality

International humanitarian law protects sick and wounded combatants, civilians, their medical caretakers and medical units from attack. The protection to which medical units are entitled does not cease unless they are used to commit acts harmful to the enemy, outside their humanitarian functions, and even then the protection does not cease until after a warning has been given and remains unheeded. The reported ECOMOG attacks on hospitals listed below would therefore, violate the rules of war.

Representatives of relief organizations confirmed that medical targets have been hit, citing the attack on the Firestone hospital in November 1992, and cases of strafing of ambulances. Among the cases of particular concern in terms of attacks on medical neutrality include:

a.   The strafing of the Firestone hospital in November 1992.
b.   The attack on Phebe Hospital on March 10, 1993. According to Dr. Walter T. Gwenigale, the Medical Director of the hospital and Bong County, a truthful, patriotic citizen of Liberia, the attack occurred at about 10:50 p.m. Two staff residences and the main hospital building were hit, as it was also the south wall of the pediatric unit. Four hospital

The key military force supporting the LNTG remained the ECOWAS Cease-Fire Monitoring Group (ECOMOG). At year's end, ECOMOG was composed of 6,000-8,000 troops—down from 12,000 in July—from six West African and East African countries, although over half of the forces was Nigerian. Initially a peacekeeping force, ECOMOG increasingly became the Interim Government's de facto army and in addition, assumed many police powers within the Monrovia perimeter.

ECOMOG was effective in its military role in maintaining relative calm within the Monrovia-Buchanan perimeter and for promptly putting down a September 15 coup attempt by a general from the Armed Forces of Liberia (AFL), who deserted in 1990, and dissident AFL supporters. Some ECOMOG soldiers have, however, also earned an unenviable reputation for a variety of illegal activities. ECOMOG reassigned several officers who were believed by outside observers to be engaged in activities detrimental to the peace process. Despite continuing criticism of ECOMOG behavior by human rights monitors, the majority of ECOMOG forces conductred themselves well during the year.

The civil war-ravaged economy, previously based primarily on iron ore, rubber, timber, diamond, and gold exports, remained stagnant. Continued disruption of economic activity, 80 to 90 percent unemployment across all sections except government, massive displacements of civilians, wanton destruction, and looting have all devastated the productive capacity of Liberia despite its rich natural endowments and potential self-sufficiency in agriculture. Massive emergency operations by the United Nations as well as by American and other Western-based relief agencies and nongovernmental organizations (NGO) continued throughout the year in ECOMOG-controlled areas.

However, they were periodically suspended in other parts of the country because of fighting, harassment, and detention of relief personnel; looting of relief agency supplies and vehicles; and occasional seemingly arbitrary security restrictions imposed by ECOMOG.

The number of human rights abuses unquestionably rose with the increased level of conflict across the country, including the massacre of over 65 civilians by inconclusively identified attackers in a Monrovia suburb on December 15. There were many credible charges that all factions flagrantly disregarded the fundamental humanitarian values. Human rights monitors also criticized ECOMOG for incidents of human rights abuse. Since 1989, when Liberia's population was recorded at 2.4 million, an estimated 300,000 persons, most of them civilians, have been killed or wounded as a result of the conflict, and close to 800,000 have taken refuge in neighboring countries. An estimated 1.1 million people have been displaced within Liberia since the war began. Approximately 130,000 Sierra Leonean refugees were also displaced repeatedly throughout the year, some landing finally within the safe haven of Monrovia. In all combat arenas, fleeing displaced persons reported villages looted and burned; use of excessive force; arbitrary detentions; impressment, particularly of children under the age of 18 into the NPFL and ULIMO-Mandingo forces; torture; individual and gang rape; summary executions; mutilations and cannibalism.

In the absence of progress on disarmament and demobilization, the United Nations Observers in Liberia (UNOMIL) began drawing down its 443-member staff in August. The fighting and looting became so ferocious in September that all humanitarian assistance outside the Tubmanburg-Monrovia-Buchanan perimeter was halted, although several NGOs resumed modest food deliveries into the interior in November and December. No progress was made in resolving outstanding incidents of past human rights abuses.

Although obeisance was paid to the 1985 Constitution, the Penal Code, and the Labor Code, because of the violent conditions obtaining up country and the overcrowding and destitute conditions for a large percentage of people living in and near Monrovia, the rights provided by these documents were largely moot.

Respect For Human Rights

According to the International Human Rights Law of the U.N., section 1, respect for the human person, including freedom from a. Political and other extrajudicial killing, indiscriminate killings increased sharply from the previous year. Although professing adherence to the rule of law, the leaders of the warring factions condoned and, in some instances, seemingly encouraged the murderous savagery that affected the civilian population more than the combatants. Despite claims to be the national army, the AFL acted as a warring faction, and AFL troops frequently engaged in a variety of human rights abuses including alleged extrajudicial killings.

Individual ECOMOG soldiers, serving a dual role as peacekeepers and peace enforcers, committed several extrajudicial killings. Such as the shooting death of a university professor on November 1 for running

The International Committee of the Red Cross (ICRC) has a family tracing program but, because of the inaccessibility of major sectors of the country throughout the year, located only a small percentage of the missing persons brought to its attention. In the wake of fighting in Bong and Maryland counties in September and October, a new wave of approximately 200,000 refugees flooded into Guinea and Cote d'Ivoire. Many of these refugees were unable to contact family members.

Torture and other cruel, inhuman, or degrading treatment or punishment were consistently carried out.

While the 1985 Constitution prohibits torture and other degrading treatment, inhuman treatment continued to be frequent. In the greater Monrovia area under ECOMOG control, with a better educated populace, a freer press, the presence of national and international human rights and humanitarian aid groups, there were fewer reports of torture than in the past.

Although the Supreme Court ruled that "trial by ordeal or sassywood"—commonly, the placement of a hot metal object on a suspect's body to induce confession in a criminal investigation—is unconstitutional, the Ministry of Internal Affairs continued to employ licensed agents who subjected suspects to this practice. A leading Monrovia-based human rights group brought suit in March seeking compensatory damages for injuries sustained by victims of the continuing traditional mode of justice, did not function because of the disruptions of the civil war. In colonial time, this sassywood method was used by men against their wives to admit to love made by the wives with another man or men.

Eyewitnesses report that ECOMOG soldiers beat and humiliated persons at ECOMOG checkpoints in Monrovia, often for curfew violations. After ECOMOG detained prominent businessman and Unity Party stalwart Peter Bonner Jallah in November 1992, for allegedly abetting the NPFL surprise attack against Monrovia, it released him in May. Jallah credibly claimed that ECOMOG and the preceding government's intelligence officers had beaten him in the head with a gun butt, administered electrical charges to his body, burned him above the genitalia areas with gasoline, and handcuffed him so tightly that he now suffers nerve damage in his hands.

NPFL fighters stripped, beat, and tortured civilians at numerous highway checkpoints in NPFL areas, usually in connection with extortion or other forms of intimidation. The NPFL reportedly detained and tortured two traditional chiefs who went to NPFL headquarters in Gbarnga in August to convince Charles Taylor to send representatives to the National Conference in Monrovia.

Roving bands of ULIMO-Krahn and ULIMO-Mandingo fighters raided villages in Cape Mount and Bomi counties, pillaging, beating, raping, and murdering civilians as they went. There are similar documented reports of primarily Liberian Peace Council (LPC) depredations in the southeastern counties. On June 28, ULIMO-Krahn fighters attacked the UNOMIL regional headquarters in Tubmanburg, beat and tortured six United Nations observers, and completely looted the head-quarters.

All warring factions regularly committed various forms of torture and mistreatment of civilians, including individual and gang rape and other violence against women.

Conditions in government jails continued to be life-threatening. Officials frequently denied prisoners medical care, family contacts, and adequate food, cells remained small, crowded, and filthy. Female prisoners were held in separate facilities for juvenile offenders. In 1994, however, the LNTG and ECOMOG regularly granted human rights groups access to prisoners in Monrovia, and these groups frequently obtained needed medical treatment for their clients. In a number of cases, the pro bono work of human rights groups and interested individuals resulted in the release of prisoners.

Especially for those whose cases were pending further examination, the conditions of detention outside Monrovia were even worse. When detained, prisoners were held in makeshift, substandard facilities and subjected to various forms of mistreatment, both physical and psychological—including beatings, rape and threatened executions. More often, however, displaced persons reported that "authorities" either let prisoners go or shot them on the spot.

Arbitrary Arrest, Detention, or Exile

Even though, the 1985 Constitution prohibits arbitrary arrest and provides for the rights of the accused, including warrants for arrests and the right of detainees either to be charged or released within 48 hours, in practice, police officers often disregarded these rights and make arbitrary arrests. Many police officers accepted bribes to arrest persons based on unsubstantiated allegations. At times they failed to inform detainees of the charges against them.

Then, often, charges went unrecorded. The LNTG Ministry of Justice moved to protect citizens' rights by issuing new procedural guidelines to the Bureau of Corrections, limiting the persons authorized to commit suspects to jail, and filing writs of dismissal for detainees who were not processed correctly.

ECOMOG soldiers played the major role in policing the greater Monrovia area, and citizens continued to turn to ECOMOG soldiers rather than the unarmed police force to arrest and detain alleged criminals. Detention by ECOMOG peace-keeping soldiers frequently did not satisfy internationally recognized standards, and there were unconfirmed reports that ECOMOG coerced confessions from suspects. ECOMOG did, however, regularly allow NGO's access to prisoners in its various detention centers. As a result of politician Peter Bonner Jallah's 18-month detention without charge, the center for law and human rights education filed a writ with the Supreme Court calling for a definition of ECOMOG's arrest and detention powers.

In its controversial September decision, the Supreme Court stated that ECOMOG "as a peace-keeping force has no legal right to arrest and detain any citizen." Toward year's end, ECOMOG and various Liberian security and law enforcement agencies established a "joint task force" intended to appropriate responsibilities and overall security duties. Although the AFL claims to be the national army, ill-disciplined AFL troops frequently committed some of the most serious human rights abuses. For example, on June 24, AFL soldiers entered the UNOMIL Demobilization Center at Schiefflin and detained the staff for three days after which they looted the center. On September 15, under the direction of a U.S. domiciled former AFL general, some AFL soldiers attempted a coup against the Government, seizing the executive mansion. ECOMOG forces swiftly put down the attempted coup and captured leader Charles Julue, 78 AFL supporters, and five civilians. After a three-week probe, ECOMOG released forty soldiers and detained thirty-eight for court-martial.

It turned the five civilians over to the civilian judiciary. The trial of the five began on October 14, but was suspended as of year's end because of procedural and security issues. The AFL court-martial of Julue, three other generals, and others began on November 16 but suffered repeated delays due to security concerns caused by dissident AFL soldiers.

While accurate arrest information was unavailable, charged and uncharged pretrial detainees in the Monrovia area formed a sizable portion of the total incarcerated population. Human rights groups reported that approximately one-third to one-half of the prisoners (average) 75% at any given moment at the Monrovia Central prison compound had not gone to trial.

Modest reforms within the court system, such as limiting the time frame for argument, reduced somewhat the backlog of cases but judicial reforms have been almost totally lacking since then. In the areas controlled by the other factions, there was little pretense of due process; swift judgement was meted out by the faction leaders. Given the continuing war, it was not possible to determine the total number of political/security detainees or political prisoners among the prisoners held by the factions.

Arbitrary interference with privacy, family, home or correspondence

While the Constitution provides for these rights, there were many serious abuses of privacy and home—including confiscation of property and failure to obtain required warrants—by the police and fighters of all the warring factions. According to the Constitution, the police must have a warrant or a reasonable belief that a crime is in progress, or is about to be committed, before entering a private dwelling. In practice, the police engaged in forced entry without a warrant to carry out arrests and investigations.

Combatants of all the warring factions looted villages during the year, with ULIMO-Krahn and ULIMO-Mandingo factions in Bomi and Cape Mount counties and LPC and NPFL fighters in southeastern counties and elsewhere drawing considerable public outrage. These forces pilfered virtually any item of value and regularly demanded scarce food and personal valuables from already impoverished residents or displaced persons, often robbing them of their clothes and physically abusing them, particularly at checkpoints.

Confiscation of private homes and vehicles was common practice. These factions also used forced entry for purposes of intimidation. For example, AFL soldiers made two raids on the Monrovia residence of a legislative representative to harass the representative for his support of the new police director. In one instance, an AFL soldier shot the representative's guard in the leg. The representative sent a formal letter to the Transitional Legislative Assembly accusing four members of the AFL high command of attempted murder.

Use of Excessive Force and Violations of Humanitarian Law in Internal Conflicts

In 1994, the warring factions inflicted considerably more harm on non-combatants than on each other. All factions indiscriminately ransacked villages and confiscated scant food supplies. They deliberately targeted, tortured, and murdered innocent civilians and regularly committed violence against women, children and the elderly.

The number and complexity of warring forces increased in 1994. In addition to Charles Taylor's NPFL in the central counties, the anti-NPFL ULIMO split in March into its two ethnic components—the ULIMO-Mandingo faction and the ULIMO-Krahn faction. While there was intra-ULIMO fighting in the Western counties, both ULIMO wings joined other groups, including the AFL, in fighting NPFL-Taylor forces in central Liberia. Made up of remnants of late President Samuel Doe's army, the AFL controlled pockets of terrain along the road to Buchanan and a few areas in and around the Firestone Plantation. The LPC, a predominantly Krahn group drawing major support from active and former AFL combatants, emerged in late 1993 and made serious inroads in 1994 against the NPFL in the south and eastern coastal region. Krahn ethnic loyalties closely linked the ULIMO-Krahn, the AFL, and the LPC. The Lofa Defense Force

(LDF) provided sporadic challenge to ULIMO-Mandingo control of the northwest.

The NPFL also suffered a schism. In August, a trio of dissident NPFL ministers, who took their LNTG cabinet seats in April, declared Charles Taylor unseated as Chairman of the NPFL's Central Revolutionary Committee. They joined other splinter groups in an anti-Taylor coalition which participated with ULIMO-Mandingo forces in a successful September attack on Taylor's Gbarnga headquarters which he reoccupied in December.

There were many incidents throughout the year in which civilians died. On June 9, LDF fighters reportedly massacred or summarily shot seventy-five civilians at Russie village near Zorzor in Lofa County. On June 22, ULIMO-Mandingos massacred nine civilians including women and children, in Brewerville, Montserrado County.

Witnesses confirmed that ULIMO troops questioned the victims about their tribal backgrounds and then killed or tortured them and threw their bodies into a well. In late August, ULIMO-Krahn fighters massacred between twenty to thirty persons in Gbesseh town, Cape Mount County. In September, there were numerous reports of a "massacre" by ULIMO-Mandingo fighters who attacked Phebe Hospital near Gbarnga, looting it and killing an unknown number of civilians, including several Phebe staff members. Subsequently, NPFL leader Charles Taylor implied the killings of civilians at Phebe Hospital had been committed by members of the NPFL. In mid-December, fighters of undetermined affiliation attacked the Paynesville suburb of Monrovia, shooting, hacking, and burning sixty-six civilians to death.

Credible reports indicated that NPFL, ULIMO-Krahn, ULIMO-Mandingo, and LPC fighters committed acts of cannibalism. In some instances, the fighters ate specific organs in the belief that it would make the fighters stronger. Human rights groups estimated that three to six percent of combatants participated. Displaced persons reported seeing severed extremities and extracted body parts, such as the heart of a Lofa County judge displayed in the streets of Voinjama after he was murdered by ULIMO-Mandingo forces. Often, it was impossible to know where the victim came from or what had happened. On September 21, a diplomat came upon an unidentified, naked and tortured corpse (pieces of rope on the deceased's wrist) along the main road through a Monrovia suburb.

The NPFL took credit for mining the Bong Mine-Kakata Road, the feeder roads to the Monrovia-Buchanan Highway, and threatened to mine the Totota-Kakata Highway if anyone attempted to save the one hundred fifty (150) thousand displaced persons in Totota. Three mine explosions elsewhere killed several civilians and two ECOMOG soldiers.

Relief organizations estimated that 1.1 million persons have been internally displaced since the war began. Most of these are dependent on humanitarian aid for survival. Upper Lofa County, for instance, where a $ 1 million staging base in Vahum had been gutted by ULIMO brigands in December 1993, remained bereft of relief operations throughout the year because the security situation was too unstable to allow relief workers to return. Fierce fighters fighting in other sectors of the country hampered humanitarian work. Faction leaders and their followers, suspicious of the possible supply of aid to the enemy, often refused to allow international and humanitarian relief agencies access beyond their checkpoints to distribute food and supplies, United Nations and relief agencies reported continuous harassment and detention of their staffs, confiscation of vehicles, and looting of food-stuffs, medical supplies, and gasoline.

In September interfactional warfare erupted in central Liberia with such renewed brutality that over 200,000 Liberians fled their homes, some to the bush and others into Guinea and the Ivory Coast, U.N. agencies and NGO's withdrew their up-country staffs after the NPFL took forty-three United Nations observers hostage in various sectors of NPFL territory and after millions of dollars of U.N. and humanitarian assistance supplies and equipment had been stolen. Assistance outside the Monrovia and Buchanan areas ground to a halt in September but resumed to a few locations at greatly reduced levels late in the year.

Various factions attacked ECOMOG peace-keeping forces throughout the year and on a number of occasions took ECOMOG soldiers hostage. At least eight ECOMOG soldiers lost their lives, and many were wounded. Similarly, the warring factions detained UNOMIL staff members and at times tortured them.

ECOMOG soldiers also inflicted suffering on the civilian population. Individual soldiers committed a number of serious illegal activities, including systematic looting not only of small, easily transportable goods but also the stripping of entire buildings for scrap to be sold abroad. Credible of—if not delivering—weapons and ammunition to the AFL, LPC, and ULIMO combatants fighting to dislodge Taylor's NPFL.

Allegedly, some ECOMOG soldiers engaged in the illegal drug trade (heroin and cocaine) and used Liberia as a transit point for drugs coming in from Nigeria and Ghana for transshipment. ECOMOG soldiers were also accused of using children as young as eight years of age as prostitutes.

Respect for Civil Liberties, Including
Freedom of Speech and Press

These freedoms are provided for in the 1985 Constitution and, with some significant limitations, citizens generally exercised these rights in Monrovia. Liberians are free to criticize the LNTG and ECOMOG, although they usually show restraint and self-censorship in favor of the temporary governments.

Due primarily to continued economic stagnation, the number of publications in Monrovia fluctuated from month to month. At year's end, there were eight privately owned newspapers in Monrovia. While a restrictive Doe-era media law providing the Ministry of Information wide discretion in licensing and regulating journalists remained on the books, official press censorship was not pervasive in Monrovia. Also, there were no newspapers forcibly closed during the year. Reflecting local opinion, most of the Monrovia press tended to be anti-NPFL; and some journalists admitted to self-censorship in favor of the interim government's case. Except for the September coup suspects, there were no known political/security detainees in the Monrovia area under LNTG jurisdiction, but it was impossible to determine the number of such detainees elsewhere in the country.

On April 5, ECOMOG released 800 NPFL fighters who had been held for over a year following their capture during the NPFL's October 1992 "operation Octopus" attack on Monrovia. UNOMIL had been charged under the 1993 Cotonou Peace Accord with supervising a demobilization figure of 3,500.

The NPFL committed repeated arbitrary detentions in its territory where martial law has been in effect since the war began, NPFL fighters had almost unbridled power to make arrests without warrants. They exercised that power often and capriciously detained persons, including U.N. military observers, on spurious grounds and without charge for periods ranging from several hours to several weeks, as in the case in May of an AFL colonel held for 1 month. The NPFL held 350 orphans, whom the NPFL abducted from Fatimah Cottage in October 1992, at Cuttington University College until the fighting, the children fled, with most of them joining the 150,000 displaced persons still held by the NPFL at year's end near Totota.

UNOMIL was able to evacuate 58 of the orphans by helicopter before the security situation made flights impossible. There were no reports of Liberians being subjected to forced political exile.

Denial of Fair Public Trial

The court structure is divided into four levels with the Supreme Court at its apex. Under the 1985 Constitution, defendants have the due process rights confirming to internationally accepted norms of fair trial. Most of these rights, however, were ignored in practice.

By 1994, all levels of the court system which had been devastated by the years of civil war were functioning in Monrovia, although erratically. While corruption and incompetent handling of cases remained a recurrent problem, some progress was made in addressing problems in the judiciary, including requiring that circuit court judges be law school graduates.

The 1994 LNTG budget included the judiciary for the first time in 4 years, which resulted in judges being given office facilities and vehicles. The Supreme Court, composed of justices nominated by the warring factions, continued to operate.

In addition to the resurrection of the modern court system, customary law was also applied in Monrovia. The Ministry of Internal Affairs subjected persons accused of occult practices and other crimes to "trial by ordeal" submitting defendants to physical pain to adjudicate guilt or innocence.

In the cases of two AFL soldiers whom a military court found guilty of murder, a leading human rights organization on their behalf appealed the death sentence to the Supreme Court. The AFL, claiming no appeal was permitted from a court-martial judgement, initially threatened to execute the prisoners but subsequently delayed action after the Supreme Court issued a restraining order. By year's end, the Ministry of Defense had not constituted an appeal board.

Although in 1991 the NPFL also partially activated the court system in areas under its control, legal and judicial protections were sparse and intermittent.

Violation Around Gbarnga

Monrovia, Liberia (Reuters)—Faction Leader Charles Taylor said on Sunday that his base in central Liberia had again come under attack from a rival militia in violation of a cease-fire accord.

"We reported this last week and there were denials here and there. Now it has happened again," Mr. Taylor told reporters traveling with him from a visit to neighboring Ivory Coast. Mr. Taylor has been very consistent and concerned about the issue of civilian population attacks in his areas from time to time, and always reports this to both the national and international medias. But, however, it seems to be as if nobody wants to listen any longer.

The Patriotic Front Leader, Mr. Charles G. Taylor, said news of fresh clashes came from commanders in his regional base in the central town of Gbarnga. They said fighting broke out when the small town of Suacoco, just south of Gbarnga, was attacked by the ULIMO militia of Alhaji Kromah. This group seems to have been practicing guerrilla warfare in the territory of the NPFL. Accordingly, battles were continuing further down the highway to Kakata; towards the capital of Monrovia. "Our information is that many people are fleeing the area," a Taylor aide told reporters.

ULIMO and Taylor's National Patriotic Front of Liberia (NPFL) are among Liberia's main factions that signed an accord in Nigeria in August to end more than five years of civil war. Mr. Taylor accused ULIMO last week of attacking NPFL positions in Gbarnga in breach of the cease-fire. ULIMO's Kromah denied the charge, blaming violence in Gbarnga on Taylor's commanders, unhappy with power-sharing under the accord.

Despite the Gbarnga clashes and a massacre of about 100 people in the area at the end of last month, the cease-fire has generally held in the West African nation. West African States trying to bring peace to the country agreed last week to raise their 7,000-strong force in Liberia to 12,000 men to police the cease-fire effectively and demobilize about 60,000 guerrillas. A six-man ruling council on which both Taylor and Kromah are members is now running Liberia until elections are held next August under terms of the peace accord.

A dozen previous accords have come to nothing in Liberia but the latest is the first to have all warlords on board. This report was made by Agence France Presse, October 16, 1995.

UN Envoy on Assessment Mission to Liberia

According to Dateline in Monrovia, October 16, 1995, the UN Secretary General for Humanitarian Affairs, Peter Hansen, Monday started a tour of Liberia by visiting rural areas in various parts of the west African country, a United Nations statement said. The UN delegation traveled to Bo Waterside at Liberia's border with Sierra Leone as well as far as Tubmanburg, Kakata and the port city of Buchanan where Hansen is expected to visit camps for refugees and displaced persons, said the statement.

Hansen, a Dane, arrived here on Sunday as the head of a UN delegation "to raise the visibility of humanitarian needs of Liberia within the international community, and to ensure that prospects for peace in

Liberia are fully supported through humanitarian action," according to the statement. He is also expected to meet with members of the Liberian collective presidency, heads of international relief organizations, and authorities of the African peacekeeping force, ECOMOG. A peace accord was signed last August by all seven parties to the war in Liberia, which has claimed more than 150,000 lives and forced 80 per cent of the country's 2.5 million inhabitants to flee their homes. The conflict has devastated Liberia, now one of the poorest countries in the world. Although it is the eleventh signed since the war was started by Charles Taylor in December 1989, the latest accord is widely believed to be the most likely to hold.

Head of Presidential Service Leads Raid on Jail: Police

According to a Dateline reporter in Monrovia, on October 18, 1995, four Liberian faction members were arrested and another injured here Friday after a raid led by the director of presidential security failed to spring three prisoners from police headquarters and ended in a shootout, police said Monday.

Police said the raid was carried out by members of the Mandingo wing of the United Liberiation Movement (ULIMO) and led by the director of the special security service at State House, Kalifala Bility, a former police officer. The special service security provides bodyguards and other forms of protection for the West African country's recently-created collective presidency, and other VIPs.

"Between five and ten militiamen stormed the police headquarters around midnight on Friday to release Wleh Myers, Beatrice Koon and Augustine Cooper from police cells," said police, who also reported the seizure of two AK-47 rifles and a machine gun. Police said they captured four of the men and that another had been severely injured. The other raiders managed to flee, and Bility was not among those arrested.

The three held at the police headquarters were detained by the security forces last Friday for their alleged connection with a "black money deal," police parlance for counterfeiting. Police said they are investigating the shooting incident.

New Fighting Reported in Liberia

According to a report from Date in Monrovia, Liberia October 15,1995, new fighting broke out on Sunday around the strategic city of Gbarnga, forcing civilians to flee and further eroding a peace accord. Gbarnga, in central Liberia, is the headquarters of the NPFL leader Charles Taylor, who is now a vice chairman on a transitional government that was inaugurated September 1, 1995. The government is supposed to oversee the peace accord and steer the country to elections next year, but recent clashes have raised fears the agreement could collapse and plunge the country back into war. Taylor accused fighters of a rival rebel faction, whose leader also sits on the new government, of starting the clashes. They occurred as Taylor wrapped up a visit to neighboring Ivory Coast, where he assured the government that Liberia's problems would not be carried across the border.

There was no word on casualties from the latest fighting. Officials in Gbarnga said that villagers had run into surrounding forests in search of safety. A dozen previous peace accords have collapsed since Liberia's war began in 1989. The latest accord was given a good chance for success, however, because of the participation of Taylor and the country's other rebel leaders and the seating of the transitional government. At least 150,000 people, most of them civilians, have died in the conflict and half the population of 2.5 million is displaced. More than 300,000 are presently living as refugees in Ivory Coast, and they say they are scared to go home in case fighting erupts again. In June, clashes between Liberian factions spread across the border killing several Ivorian villagers, straining relations between the countries and prompting Taylor's visit to Abidjan.

Before leaving Sunday, he joined with other Liberian and Ivorian representatives in signing an agreement to strengthen security on the border to prevent future cross-border raids. Which somewhat indicates that Taylor is out there for something for the Liberian people's future, which others might never understand until the future brings it on shore

ECOWAS Commanders End Emergency Meeting; More Troops Pledged

According to GBC radio, Accra, in English 1800 gmt 11 October, 1995, [32] Text of report by Ghanaian radio on 11th Oct.—An emergency meeting of ECOWAS Economic Community of West African States chiefs of staff has ended in Monrovia with pledges for more troop contributions by member states to the ECOMOG ECOWAS Cease-fire Monitoring Group peacekeeping force in Liberia. The two-day meeting was attended by Ghana, Nigeria, the Gambia, Sierra Leone and Guinea. The others were Mali, Togo, Cote d'Ivoir, Burkina Faso, Benin, Niger and 004Ciberia. Nigeria pledged to increase its troops by two more battalions. Cote d'Ivoire,

Burkina Faso and Togo pledged to contribute troops but the rest promised assistance to various aspects of the peace implementation process. Last week, the ECOWAS chairman, President John Jerry Rawlings, called for total involvement of ECOWAS members in the Liberian peace process, warning that lack of the required troop strength and logistics threatens to delay its implementation. A source at the meeting said the chiefs of staff are convinced that their governments will respond positively to the request by ECOWAS Chairman to whom they expressed gratitude for his personal leadership and efforts at ensuring peace in Liberia.

ECOWAS says it needs to raise troop level to 12,000 men, up from the current 3,000, and an estimated 110m dollars to ensure effective nationwide deployment to accomplish the task of disarmament, demobilization and reintegration of the combatants as provided for under the Abuja Accord.

The ECOWAS chiefs of staff also met members of Liberia's Council of State with whom they held lengthy discussions on the peace process. They also visited parts of the country to acquaint themselves with the deployment of ECOMOG contingents. The special representative of ECOWAS chairman in Liberia, Dr. Victor Gbeho, said the extras were particularly useful for those whose countries are at the moment not contributing troops to ECOMOG. He said the meeting concluded on a high note of satisfaction with the work of ECOMOG.

Meanwhile, a delegation dispatched by President Rawlings has been holding consultations with the Liberian leadership, as well as representatives of international organizations, to assess progress made since the cease-fire went into effect and the aftermath of the installation of the new council of state. The delegation led by a member of the council of state, Capt. Kojo Tsikata, held talks with the collective leadership and met individual council members. The delegation also held talks with members of the United States Inter-Agency Task Force to Liberia which, over the past week, assessed possible areas of the U.S. government's assistance to enhance the peace process. From Liberia, the delegation will proceed to Gambia and Burkino Faso for consultations with Presidents Yhya Jammeh and Blaise Compaore on the effective implementation of the peace process before returning home.

DISCRIMINATION BASED ON RACE, SEX, RELIGION, DISABILITY, LANGUAGE, OR SOCIAL STATUS

THE 1985 CONSTITUTION prohibits discrimination based on ethnic background, race, sex, creed, place of origin, or political opinion, but discrimination exists in fact and, in some cases, in law.

Women

The status of women varies by region, ethnic group, and religion. Before the outbreak of the civil war, women held one-quarter of the professional and technical occupations available in Monrovia. Some women currently hold skilled jobs in government including in the cabinet, legislature, and judiciary. On the whole, however, the lot of women deteriorated dramatically with the onset of war, the closing of many schools, and the loss of their traditional role in production, distribution, and sale of foodstuffs. In the past three years, several women's organizations formed in Monrovia and Gbarnga to advance family welfare issues, to help promote political reconciliation, and to assist in rehabilitation rehabilitating former combatants as well as civilian victims of war. In urban areas, where traditional customs are stronger, a wife is normally considered the property of her husband and his clan and usually is not entitled to inherit from her husband.

Women in most rural areas do much farm labor and have only limited access to education. In the massive violence inflicted on civilians during the conflict, women suffered the gamut of abuses. Even prior to the war, domestic violence against women was extensive, but the government, the courts, the media, and women's groups never seriously addressed the issue. There are several NGO's in Monrovia and Buchanan which have developed programs for treating abused women and girls and increasing their awareness of their human rights.

Children

In the civil war, the various sides have given almost no attention to the welfare of children whose education and nurturing have been seriously disrupted. Many who were disabled, orphaned, abandoned, or "lost" during a military attack on their homes or villages, reportedly accepted the protection and sustenance that joining a faction brought. Both the NPFL and the ULIMO-Mandingos recruited and trained children as cooks, spies, errand runners, guards, and in many instances combatants. There were no precise figures on the number of child soldiers, but some sources estimated that ten percent of the forty thousand to sixty thousand combatants are under fifteen years of age. Many children are substance abusers and depend upon the factions for supply. As a result, children have become both victims and abusers in the conflict. Many suffer from post-traumatic stress disorder. Some NGOs have initiated small retraining and rehabilitation programs for a limited number of former child fighters.

International health experts have condemned child combatant training programs, especially, their physical, psychological and emotional aspects; it is damaging to the child, young women who are directly involved in the program. In some instances, female health professionals in the areas have successfully participated in the ceremony to the extent of providing comfort and emotional support. The training primarily involved young girls and boys in the northern, western, and central regions, particularly in rural areas. According to an independent expert in the institution, the percentage of children (females) who have forcibly undergone this training may be as high as sixty percent. Although there was one newspaper report of a failed attempt to force a girl in Gbarnga to undergo the training, it was difficult to confirm the extent to which this procedure was continued in 1994 by Liberia's uprooted, displaced, and often inaccessible population. The most extreme form of forceful combatant training was not practiced in Liberia prior to the civil war in 1989.

National/Racial/Ethnic Minorities

Although the Constitution bans ethnic discrimination, it also provides that only "persons who are negroes or negroes' descendants" may be citizens or own land, thus denying full rights to many who were born or lived most of their lives in Liberia. There has been no legislative initiative to repeal this racial test. The 1975 Economic "Liberianization" law prohibits foreign ownership of certain businesses, such as travel agencies, retail gasoline stations, and beer and soft drink distributors. This law resulted in the rejection of several foreign-owned business proposals.

The roots of the civil conflict can be found in the historical division between the America-Liberian minority, who, despite representing less than five percent of the population, for over one hundred and fifty years dominated the political, economic, and cultural life of the country, and the indigenous ethnic groups. The latter frequently complained of government discrimination in many areas, such as access to education and civil service jobs and to infrastructure development.

The authoritarian military-based regime established after the 1980 coup mounted by Sergeant Doe and other AFL noncommissioned officers progressively exacerbated ethnic tensions while subverting the democratic reforms embodied in the 1985 Constitution. During the Doe regime, resentment grew over domination of government by Doe's ethnic group, the Krahns, which represent approximately four percent of the population. Throughout the civil war, the factions have used an executed individual's language to identify ethnicity and often summarily executed those from groups considered hostile. The ULIMO faction split in March along Krahn-Mandingo lines and fought each other and the NPFL. The NPFL, supported by the Gio and Mano groups, waged war against four preponderantly ethnically constituted factions, three of them Krahn: the predominately Krahn AFL troops in and around Monrovia, the Krahn LPC along the southern coast and north into (Krahn) Grand Gedeh County, and the ULIMO-Krahns in Bong County.

The ULIMO-Mandingos made incursions against the NPFL in Bong County and from early September until December held control of Gbarnga, the NPFL stronghold.

Other journalists asserted that public calls by IGNU and subsequently LNTG officials for a "more responsible" press had a chilling effect on journalistic freedom. At times, government officials and senior ECOMOG officers, offended by articles, insisted on meeting privately with journalists. Perhaps most chilling were the reported threats to individual journalists by persons claiming to represent one or another of the warring factions. After a group of citizens from ULIMO territory published a statement in Monrovia that ULIMO should relinquish control of the western counties to the LNTG, the ULIMO leadership threatened physical harm to journalists who published articles making such suggestions.

There was no overt general attempt to censor the press, such as the mid-1993 directive from IGNU that journalists submit all "war related" stories to the Ministeries of Information and Justice for clearance on national security grounds. At that time, the Press Union of Liberia (PUL) and newspaper publishers objected to the measure as a prior restraint, but the PUL and IGNU later compromised on guidelines for military reporting.

Those guidelines continued in effect and undoubtedly constituted part of the basis for self-censorship. Except when fighting became too widespread, international journalists were able to visit contested zones and to file reports without official censorship. Because of the fighting, journalists from Monrovia cannot report on events in NPFL areas where I was residing at the time, and vice versa.

Outside Monrovia, residents of Liberia exercised extreme care in their criticism of the various factions. Although NPFL leader Mr. Charles G. Taylor affirmed publicly on several occasions his support of free speech, citizens in his area were subject to sanctions for criticizing the NPFL. There were two pro-NPFL newspapers intermittently published in NPFL territory, but no newspapers were printed in ULIMO or LPC controlled areas. Both NPFL papers were initially denied permission to circulate in Monrovia by the LNTG because they were not one of the papers legally "registered". LNTG officials seized copies of one of the papers on at least one occasion.

ECOMOG, IGNU, and subsequently the LNTG supported a radio station (ELBC) which broadcast pro-government (and at times sycophantic) programming throughout 1994. Many credible journalists alleged substantial censorship of ELBC. A privately owned radio station began broadcasting from Monrovia in October 1993, but limited its news and commentary in order to avoid possible governmental interference. The NPFL continued to operate intermittently at least one radio station, which uncritically supported Charles Taylor.

The University of Liberia functioned throughout 1994 despite some delays caused by financial problems. Academic freedom was generally respected, although the University authorities and most of the student body criticized pro-NPFL expression.

Freedom of Peaceful Assembly and Association

The Constitution provides for the rights of peaceful assembly and association. ECOMOG, apparently with full IGNU agreement, imposed a nighttime curfew in Monrovia from 7 p.m. to 7 a.m. after the NPFL attack in 1992;

the curfew continued in force. ECOMOG soldiers enforced the measure strictly and arrested numerous persons for noncompliance. ECOMOG periodically meted out corporal punishment to repeat curfew violators.

The LNTG and ECOMOG permitted political parties and other groups to organize freely and hold public meetings in Monrovia, but ECOMOG did prohibit an outdoor peace rally in July and generally discouraged parades or demonstrations for security reasons. The NPFL and ULIMO-Mandingo forces severely restricted freedom of assembly and association in their areas. In other factions' areas, residents felt intimidated and did not attempt demonstrations.

Freedom of Religion

The 1985 Constitution recognizes freedom of religion as a fundamental right, and Liberia has no established state religion. There was no evidence of systematic violation of religious freedom by warring factions, but there were isolated and sometimes violent incidents of religious repression by local fighters, especially by Muslim ULIMO-Mandingo forces.

Freedom of Movement Within the Country, Foreign Travel, Emigration, and Repatriation

The Constitution provides for freedom of movement throughout Liberia as well as the right to leave or enter the country at will. ECOMOG monitored freedom of movement at checkpoints within Monrovia and around its perimeter.

Factional fighting interferred with freedom of movement, ranging from resettlement of displaced persons to ordinary commerce and travel. ECOMOG restricted the movement of civilians, humanitarian aid and staffers at various times throughout the year. All factions impeded the movement of relief workers and supplies and extorted, humiliated, and harassed citizens at checkpoints and makeshift barricades.

Of the estimated population of almost 2.7 million at the end of 1994, approximately 1.1 million Liberians have been internally displaced since 1990, and 776,000 were refugees in neighboring West African countries, many out of fear of ethnic persecution. The number of refugees fluctuated depending on the intensity and proximity of the fighting to population centers. Many of the displaced went to Monrovia, including the 6,000 former refugees who returned to Liberia, reportedly because of the security and more reliable relief supplies.

There were approximately 130,000 Sierra Leonean refugees in Liberia as the civil war spilled over into Sierra Leone. Many Sierra Leoneans suffered mistreatment by both ULIMO factions and NPFL as they were displaced from camps in Western counties and made their way to camps in Lofa County (where approximately 70,000 reside) and camps in and around Monrovia.

Respect for Political Rights; The Right of Citizens to Change their Government

Despite constitutional and statutory provisions for free and fair elections, Liberians could not exercise the right to change their government. Implementation of the July 1993 Cotonou Accord and follow-up September 1994 Akosombo Agreement lagged as the factions continued to argue at year's end over the detailed arrangements and timetable for seating a new transitional government, disarmament, and demobilization. The December Akosombo Clarification Agreement postponed elections until November 1995 and the installation of an elected government until January 1996.

The LNTG installed in March 1994 is a weak transitional Government comprised of representatives of the signatories to the Cotonou Accord—IGNU, NPFL, and ULIMO. There is a five person Council of State appointed by the signatory factions, a thirty-five member Transitional Legislative Assembly (TLA) also appointed by the factions, and the judiciary. At the end of the year, it remained to be seen whether the factions could implement the new LNTG called for in the December 21 Accra Agreements.

There are no restrictions in law on the participation of women in politics; in practice, two women hold cabinet-level positions in the LNTG, and a few hold positions in the legislature and judiciary. Over all numbers of women in the LNTG and the various political parties are small.

Governmental Attitude Regarding International and Non-Governmental Investigation of Alleged Violations of Human Rights

The Interim Governments have permitted domestic and international groups to operate freely. The few domestic human rights organizations are relatively new and underfunded but made progress improving their influence, visibility, and performance.

There were no domestic human rights organizations outside the ECOMOG-controlled areas due to the warring factions' hostility to such organizations.

Religious Minorities

While the law prohibits religious discrimination, there were claims of discrimination in practice. Some Muslims, who represent a growing share of the population, believe that Liberia's secular culture gives preference to Christianity in civic ceremonies and observances, and that discrimination spills over into areas of individual opportunity and employment. The Muslim education system stresses religious as opposed to skills-based learning.

As a result, the authorities frequently by-passed Muslims for the highly sought-after technical and bureaucratic jobs available in government. In addition, many Liberian Muslims believe that their access to jobs and roles in public life are restricted by an anti-Muslim bias in many sectors of Liberian society with a predominantly Christian education.

People With Disabilities

The protracted civil war has produced a large number of persons with permanent injuries in addition to persons disabled from other causes. There is no legal discrimination against the disabled, but in practice they do not enjoy equal access to education, employment, and scant social services. There are no laws mandating accessibility to public buildings or services.

Worker Rights and the Right of Association

The 1985 Constitution states that workers, except military and police, have the right to associate in trade unions. However, as with virtually all other organized activity in the counrtry, unions disappeared during the height of the 1989-90 war. With the signing of the July 1993 Cotonou Peace Accord, many industries planned to resume, and affected unions began reorganizing and attempted to locate members. However, union efforts to reorganize generally faltered in 1994 as factional fighting increased. The most active organization was the ship workers' union.

The 1985 Constitution is silent on the right to strike. While the labor code provides for this right, the Doe government issued a "no-strike decree" in 1980. Governments up to 1980 intimidated labor officials, assuring a generally docile work force and labor environment. Neither of the subsequent IGNU and LNTG Legislative assemblies repealed or affirmed the no-strike decree, which was not challenged in 1994 as there were no strikes.

During the year, the LNTG took no discriminatory actions against organized labor. In 1990, the U.S. Government suspended Liberia's eligibility for trade benefits under the Generalized System of Preferences because of its violations of workers rights. Labor unions have traditionally affiliated freely with international labor groups.

The Right to Organize and Bargain Collectively

With the important exception of civil servants, workers (including employees of public corporations and autonomous agencies) have the right to organize and bargain collectively. In the past, labor and employers negotiated agreements freely without government intereference. In 1994, those rights were largely moot because of the lack of economic enterprise, especially in Monrovia where only a few businesses resumed operation, usually with reduced staffing. There were no formal mechanisms in place for resolving complaints of discrimination against union workers.

There was no activity in Liberia's one export processing zone (EPZ) which has been inoperative since 1990 when fighting reached the free port of Monrovia.

Prohibition of Forced or Compulsory Labor

The Constitution prohibits forced labor, but even before the civil-war local authorities widely ignored this prohibition in rural areas where farmers were pressured into providing free labor on "community projects," which often benefited only local leaders. The warring factions used forced labor during the fighting, especially for moving equipment or supplies.

According to credible reports, ULIMO-Mandingo fighters also used Sierra Leonean refugees to acquire food for them, causing the flight and repatriation of approximately five thousand Sierra Leoneans from Vahun, Lofa County.

Minimum Age for Employment of Children

Under the Doe Government, the law prohibited employment of children under age sixteen during school hours in the wage sector. This law is still technically in effect, but there is no enforcement. Even earlier, enforcement by the Ministry of Labor was limited, and small children continued to assist their parents as vendors in local markets and on family subsistence farms. This practice persisted in 1994, particularly in those areas where school had been closed because of the war. During the conflict, the NPFL and ULIMO-Mandingos recruited young children as soldiers, many of whom had been orphaned; some were less than twelve years of age. Many of these children, especially in the NPFL remained under arms in 1994.

Acceptable Condition of Work

The Labor Code provides for a minimum wage, paid leave, severance benefits, and safety standards. Before the economy collapsed, the legal minimum wage varied according to profession but did not generally provide a decent standard of living for a worker and family. The minimum wage for agricultural workers was approximately ninety cents per day, with industrial workers receiving three or four times that amount. Often workers were forced to supplement their incomes through other activities to maintain a minimal standard of living. Those not displaced turned to subsistence farming. The minimum wage was not enforced adequately by the Ministry of Labor.

The Labor Code provides for a 48-hour, six day regular workweek with a 30 minute rest period for every five hours of work. The six-day workweek may extend to 56 hours for service occupations and to 72 hours for miners, with overtime pay beyond 48-hours. In view of the low level of economic activity during 1994, most employers ignored these various regulations, and there was very little attempt at enforcement in the country.

Prior to 1990, there also had been government-established health and safety standards, enforced in principle by the Ministry of Labor. Workers did not have a legal right to remove themselves from dangerous situations.

With the civil war in Liberia in its sixth year and nearly two million either dead or displaced, Edward O'Loughlin reports from Monrovia on the lawlessness in the country and the impotency of the United Nations in an affair which threatens the stability of its West Africa neighbors.

History records that the modern state of Liberia was carved from the inhospitable coast of the Gulf of Guinea by freed American slaves who, for much of the past two centuries, were barely in contact with the "natives" of the pagan interior.

Now, 170 years later, Liberia is back where it started, only worse. After five years of often surreal conflict, the coast is once more cut off from the interior, where the old tribal structures have been replaced by guerilla factions which have looted the country bare.

Since the current civil war broke out in 1989, up to ten percent of Liberia's two million inhabitants are thought to have died, while more than 1.2 million are refugees or internally displaced.

There is no government, and no law outside Monrovia and the coastal towns where the peace is vigorously kept by troops from ECOMOG, a Nigerian dominated military observer group drawn from the Economic Community of West African States (ECOWAS).

Having failed in Rwanda and fled Somalia, the United Nations is fading in Liberia. The United Nations has a small military observer group on the ground but otherwise seems content to leave peacekeeping to ECOMOG, which for three years has been actively involved in the fight against the main guerrilla faction, led by Charles G. Taylor.

The main United Nations relief agencies are all present but seem slumped in torpor. One official at the United Nations High Commissioner for Refugees office admitted, for example, it is more than six months since anyone from the UN has laid eyes on sixty-five thousand refugees from the spill-over conflict in neighboring Sierra Leone. The refugees are in the remote Lofa County, where cholera is reported to have killed several hundred people in recent weeks.

There are more than 120,000 Sierra Leonean refugees scattered around Liberia and, thanks to looting and sporadic hold-ups by faction fighters, the UNHCR which has a mandate to look after them, is in contact with fewer than half of them. The last visit to the Upper Lofa refugees was made late last year by the U.N.'s one and only helicopter.

So who is looking after the much larger numbers of Liberian "displaced persons," who are camped beside the Sierra Leonean "refugees"? "That's a very good question," the official muses.

The main armed faction is the National Patriotic Front of Liberia led by Charles G. Taylor, a former minister in the government of the late dictator, Samuel Doe, formerly a 28-year-old master sergeant in the Liberian army. Doe became president in 1980 by staging a coup and killing president William R. Tolbert, Jr. thus ending over a century of domination by the Americo-Liberian True Whig Party.

One of Doe's first acts was to invite the press to witness the mass executions of key figures from the old regime, and his soldiers, mostly fellow members of the Krahn tribe, were accused of using great brutality—including ritual cannibalism in suppressing dissent.

Liberia had been run as a de-facto United States colony since the 1920s, when the country was all but taken over by Firestone Rubber Company to secure strategic rubber supplies for the U.S. Yet American support for the True Whig elite and the evident brutality of the new regime did not prevent the Reagan administration for adopting Doe as a Cold War ally.

U.S. direct aid from 1980 to 1987 totalled 500 million more than the total for the rest of sub-Saharan Africa and was only cut after the massive corruption became more than the U.S. and the International Monetary Fund could bear.

When it finally came, Taylor's invasion enjoyed at least tacit support from the government of the neighboring Ivory Coast and most of his soldiers were drawn from the Mano and Gio ethnic groups along the Ivorian frontier.

Their opponents in the Armed Forces of Liberia were mostly Krahn like Doe, and the civil war quickly degenerated into an ethnic shambles as gunmen from both sides massacred whole villages belonging to rival groups.

In Monrovia, individuals and households were frequently targets by factions as forces loyal to Taylor and a breakaway faction led by Prince Yormie Johnson closed in on Doe's last stronghold. Doe was killed by Johnson in 1990. When Taylor launched "Operation Octopus" to take the city in 1992 this offensive was halted by ECOMOG troops which have since driven Taylor's forces back to the Ivorian frontier in the east and into Nimba County in the far north.

Deployed in 1990, as a peacekeeping force, ECOMOG has become a de-facto party to the conflict and many suspect that George Boley's recently formed Liberian Peace Council, which holds the southern frontier with the Ivory Coast, is a front of ECOMOG.

The powerful United Liberation Movement of Liberian for Democracy, a mutation of the old Doe alliance, last year split into warring Krahn and Mandingo factions. The Mandingo faction, led by Alhaji G. V. Kroma, is believed to be the most powerful group in the country besides NPFL.

Foreign observers say there is no apparent chain of command and the gunmen manning the road blocks outside Monrovia, some as young as eight years old, are motivated more by the opportunity to pillage and rape rather than any political or even tribal loyalty.

With the Cold War over, the U.S. (the de-facto colonial power) has lost interest in Liberia. For its fellow western African states, however, Liberia represents a serious threat of destabilization. In retaliation for Sierra Leone's role in ECOMOG, Charles Taylor had been aiding the Revolutionary United

Front under Foday Sankoh, which invaded Sierra Leone from Liberia in 1991 and, as far as anyone can tell, controls much of the country.

In the east, the war spilled over into the Ivory Coast two weeks ago when Liberian Peace Council fighers clashed with Ivorian border guards and troops. Dozens of Liberian refugees are believed to have been killed in subsequent Ivorian "security operations."

To the north, Guinea feels especially vulnerable to destabilization and Guinean elements are said to be favoring ULIMO's predominantly Mandingo faction.

The main foreign player in Liberia is Nigeria, which contributed the majority of ECOMOG's troops. While Nigeria seems to have originally deployed the troops in the interests of peace and stability for the past five years the soldiers have settled in and acquired a reputation for racketeering, brutality and arrogance.

The Nigerians effectively run Monrovia. A number of local and foreign observers told the Irish Times they believe local Nigerian troops are deliberately prolonging the war. The soldiers' interests are not necessarily the interests of Nigeria; however, and there are signs that Nigeria's military dictator, General Sani Abacha, may be tiring of the stalemate in Liberia.

After seven months of deadlock over what role Charles Taylor should play in a new six-member executive council intended to pave the way towards peace, Abacha surprised the region last month when he invited Taylor—hitherto shunned and vilified as a troublemaker—for private talks in Nigeria. The Nigerian commander of ECOMOG was not invited.

With the United Nations threatening to shut down UNOMIL if things have not improved by September 15th, there is fresh impetus for a settlement. The warring factions are to meet again in Accra, Ghana, later this month and, with the substance of the Abacha Taylor talks unknown, there is renewed speculation that, after five years of war, Taylor might still come out on top.

Liberian Militia Leader Says No Election in September 1994

In Conakry, Guinea, June 18, 1994, Liberian militia leader Alhaji Kromah said on Saturday that there was no chance that the West African country could meet a September 7 United Nations deadline for elections.

Speaking to Reuters during a visit to neighboring Guinea Kromah said that before polls could open the ECOMOG African peacekeeping force must be restructured and a multi-tribal national Liberian army formed.

"September is no longer practicable. With all the problems still to be solved I don't see elections taking place in less than a year," he said.

Kromah's ULIMO militia is one of three civil war foes that signed a peace accord last July, pledging to disarm and join a power-sharing government while arranging elections.

ULIMO—itself split between Kromah's supporters and dissident Krahn tribesmen—has yet to fill two of its seven allotted cabinet seats. Disarmament never really got under way and new fighting groups have emerged since the July treaty.

The U.N. Security Council is to review progress, or lack of it, by June 30 and has said adherence to the September election deadline will be a key factor in deciding whether to keep United Nations military observers in Liberia.

Kromah and former rebel leader Charles Taylor both accuse the dominant Nigerian contingent in the 13,000-strong ECOMOG of aiding their enemies. But while Taylor wants all the Nigerians out, Kromah asks that individual units which he says aided ULIMO dissidents be withdrawn from his territory.

He said his men still held two Nigerian soldiers out of 26 captured with Krahn fighers during fighting between rival ULIMO wings around ture happiness and well-being cannot be attained without the overturning or eradication of the warring factions and the restoration of peace and democracy with full national rights and equality for all.

With God above to confirm all rights, we appeal for the support and encouragement of all those Liberians and friends who seek and hope for the happiness and freedom of the Liberian people. May the Lord bless Liberians everywhere in the world today and restore peace and democracy in the nation.

Long live the President, Congress, Government, and the people of the United States of America, and save the nation. May God bless the great world body—the UNITED NATIONS, our source of hope and trust for redemption in time to come. We can proudly say that America is our "Earthly Heaven," Washington D.C. is the Holy place, the White House is the most Holy place for us. President Clinton has fought and still fights against the devil to save the children of God from all atrocities, regardless of race and nationality.

Liberians are very proud of the United States of America because it is a Great Nation which the entire universe looks up to for safety. Our founding fathers left this great "Power" to find us a home in Africa. As one of them, Elijah Johnson of Virginia, said, "I have sought a home, and here have I found one, and here will I remain".

Liberians walk throughout Africa as descendants of free slaves from North America. Other African countries have tried to reach America through Liberia in times past. Sooner or later, nobody will be allowed to enter America through Liberia. Our leaders must come to learn justice and fair-play in the United States of America to protect their land. America, the best she may ever do for Africa is to help train prospective African leaders and instill in them the importance of the principles of democracy.

Consistent donations of any kind to Africa is never the solution to the problems of Africa. Injustice must be eradicated within time. Injustice was born in Africa, and then spread through Europe and unto the New World (America). We must, first of all, address this problem by calling it by the actual name. Every day we hear of "Domestic Violence, Drug Abuses, etc." The majority of these enemies of civilization and modern life come as a result of "Injustice."

BORBOR JOHN
AND THE BUCKET BRIGADE

JOSEPH JENKINS ROBERTS, primus Inter pares, woke up one night and, haunted by what he thought was an ominous dream, alarmed his wife Ann and his entire household. Ann looked and thought she saw men and women, boys as well as girls, with buckets and pans and whatever they could find, searching for water all over the place.

In old, abandoned wells and water holes from Bill Diggs' well and old-lady Tetia Johnson's on Broad Street, down to Julia Duncan's on Sekou Toure Ave. and wells out around Cooper's farm. You could see them moving up on Snapper Hill, then back on Crown Hill; some descending to Sinkor, Congotown, Paynesville and beyond to Bushrod Island and anywhere the "running water" had reached, because the invading boys had jammed its source in White Plains.

Turning the hands of progress back to the old days . . . Oh! my loving Ann, what is this I am seeing? You mean to tell me that all our labor is in vain? To build a great nation that all would be proud of, but from what I see, we have gone back to the Dark Ages.

Lord, help me, this is too much for me to bear. President Roberts calls from the balcony of the old State House: I say Sarah, Maima, Dugbormah, Assatu, tell Ciata, Garmai, Krugbo, Monah and all the girls in the kitchen that there is no cooking in this house today and no where else.

For we all must fervently pray for the nation that the good God of Heaven will hear us in tears and hunger and heal our land. By the way, call Garsua, Sumo, Mamadee and all the boys in quarter one; call Ninbly, Darkina, Boima and Nete-sie. Let Nayou, Charlie, Yeduo, Dwenyan and Big Daddy Fahn go quickly and fetch my colleagues. I mean Stephen Allen Benson, Warner and Payne, with E. J. Roye, Gardiner and A. F. Russell. Tell H. R.

W. Johnson, Cheeseman and W. D. Coleman to come. Also G. W. Gibson, Oldman Arthur Barclay and Daniel Howard. I beg them to come and sit with the latest arrivals like Charlie King, Eddie Barclay, Tubman, Tolbert and Samuel K. Doe, to hear from them what's been going on down there.

For the shocking news we hear is enough to scatter a giant's heart. Pa Darkena begins: The things we saw down there our mouths can't tell all. Not only are your people searching for water all over the place, the people are suffering, starving, sick, and dying like flies. There are dead, unburied bodies thrown all over the place.

Your people live on wild leaves and greens of all descriptions. And the popular greens are "BORBOR JOHN," "CHICKEN GREEN," "FIVE FINGERS," etc. Wild eddoes, palm kernels, "Kiss me." You name them. Beer seeds, chicken feeds, for days that's all your people eat. Dogs and cats are exterminated; for what, it's anybody's guess.

Imagine, Pa, twenty persons to one cup of rice, it's fifteen to twenty dollars a cup.

Three little string—don't call them cassava—are sold for five dollars. Farina is sold from one thousand to five thousand dollars per bag, because it is ten to fifteen dollars a pint. A lump of sugar, a pod of pepper, a pod of palm nuts is twenty-five cents each. Pa, for days your people also live only on tea and often times without sugar. Your once lusty, vivacious people now look like ghosts from Palm Grove. Something has to be done and soon, or Liberia, the sweet land of liberty, might soon vanish from the comity of nations.

Thank you, boys, for this useful information. It will help greatly when the Council of Elders meets, President Roberts assures. But Pa, that is not all, Old Darkena continues. Your people are walking and tracking wherever they have to go from Cape Mount to Monrovia; from Bomi Hills to Grand Bassa. They walk from Kakata to Gbarnga, Sanniquellie and just about everywhere.

The civil war broke up or grounded nearly all of the means of transportation. The people rely on what was once known in your days as the "FOOT-MOBILE" or "ANKLE EXPRESS." But thank God the Wheelbarrow Vans are back on the scene. They transport load, human beings and help with others.

President J. J. Roberts

Good evening, gentlemen, thanks for your presence. The meeting will be brief but certainly urgent, and important. It's all about our dear nation—Liberia, which we left many years ago. We are all alarmed and concerned about that calamitous civil war down there that is destroying our nation, its people and all it represents. President King, you were ushered in during the thirties; tell us what really happened. Would you have any clue as to what led to the problem down there since you left the scene three decades ago?

President C. D. B. King

Distinguished gentlemen, I am happy to be among you. It all looks like a dream, but certainly, gentlemen, you must have heard about Firestone, and rubber, the backbone of the Liberian economy for many years; about Booker T. Washington Institute, electricity, roads and other such development projects. These were some major goals and achievements during my period of service. But we went unexpectedly wrong somewhere as they sometimes do in human affairs, so that the people, the real depository of power, and our sovereignty, with importance though, demanded my resignation, which I tendered with little delay and turned over to Eddie. I mean, Edwin Barclay. As to the actual cause of the conflict down there, I don't have the slightest idea.

President Edwin Barclay

Honorable gentlemen, there were no secrets about my monumental tasks, when I assumed the leadership of our beloved nation. Those were different years internationally as well as internally. The oppression was raging and commodities were extremely scarce. But, in spite of all the adversaries and hard times, I did my best to keep our ship of state afloat. My successor, Mr. Tubman, and I even met the eminent Franklin Roosevelt, and planned the course our country should take in many areas of development: water, improved roads, airports, seaports, and other infrastructures—water and sewer plants and all that goes with modern living. It breaks my heart to learn that brutal civil war left the people bereft of most of the things that make life comfortable. With these brief sentiments, gentlemen, let me present the illustrious Tubman.

President Tubman

Thank you gentlemen, thank you Eddie. All that my predecessor said about our blue print and agenda for development are correct. I carried them out to the minutest degree and even beyond. But, of all my development programs I esteemed most my effort to unify the people of the land in one homogenous whole. For unless this was achieved, all our efforts at development would be in vain. For there was too much talk of "Country-Men," "Congo Man," "Americo-Liberian," etc. For a divided people are weak, destructive, and easily defeated. It saddens my heart to know that, during the years of his leadership, I mean the brief ten years of our colleague, Samuel K. Doe, the first indigenous son ever to assume the presidency of our land—Liberia, the nation degenerated in the worst quagmire of tribalism, the likes of which we have never seen nor heard before.

Plunging this nation into the deadliest civil war more than strife that we never dreamed of. That almost brought this glorious land of liberty to near collapse. Until troops of names five African nations under the zeal of ECOWAS hurriedly came to our rescue to avert the demise of our cherished Republic, the U.S.A., not forgetting the benevolence of the United Nations, other foreign governments and several relief agencies. My heart is too full of grief. So let me stop here and present the energetic, faithful and loyal President Tolbert.

President Tolbert

My most distinguished sires, let the inimitable Tubman speak for me. For nineteen long years, I served under Tubman as his vice president, faithfully and honestly. I stood by him in difficult times and shared his joys in happy times. Not one day did I ever undermine him or betray his trust until the good Lord Himself saw fit to summon him home.

At which time I succeeded him as our law decrees. I inspired our people to achieve to the limits of their abilities. To rely on themselves, and only themselves, for the development of their land. I pursued and performed my duties with unfailing zeal until seventeen young men under the cover of the night invaded the Executive Mansion and abridged my life and work. But they failed to realize that the day before, I had fasted all day as it was National Fast and Pray Day; a double portion of the Lord's blessings I had therefore embraced. And so in just ten brief years, like the Ghost of Caesar, the Lord avenged my death when I met most of my adversaries at "Philipi".

President Doe

Honored Sires, sages of the land, I greet you with reverence and in deep humility. Of all the Chief Magistrates of this land that ever tasted death, I appear before you as the youngest but with the most experience. I felt the horrors of death even before the breath left my body, for my toes and fingers were cruelly manicured and my ears torturously clipped. I endured the excruciating pains of death, but thank God, soon after, death was induced. My body was then mockingly laid in state, and in the nude (not covered by clothing, or a drape) while thousands of my fellow countrymen filed past and pretended their last respects. I was often misled by many of my so called government workers in Liberia.

They always fooled me in making vital decisions on behalf of the people. Injustice was the song of the day; but I was often told that everything was okay, even if they were wrong and hurt the Liberian people. The only solution which they gave me was to jail my opponents.

Now I know that my opponents were the best advisers I ever had during my ten year term of office. I am now advising anybody who wishes to follow me hereafter, to always listen to your opponents instead those who claim to love you; they will always deceive you and mislead you.

When the rebel soldiers came as close as Grand Bassa County and Margibi County, I decided to turn over the country to the people, at which time the Minister of Information and Tourism told me not to resign; Taylor was never the man who elected me, rather it was the Liberian people. In any case, I was childish enough to listen to this man.

Ninety-five percent of my area was seized from me by the rebel forces; yet I was crazy enough to insist on fighting them. I was asked by the American government to leave the country at this time, but I stupidly refused depending on my cabinet ministers. At last, they all fled and escaped into the United States and left me in the heat of the night. Certainly, "pride goeth before destruction, and haughty spirit before a fall." But to make a long story short, I beg your pardon for all my misdeeds. I tried the best I possibly could to govern this nation in the manner I thought best, but the fortunes and follies of youth pervaded my head. I listened to my head instead of my heart. I, therefore, admonish all those that would come after me never to unreasonably challenge, flout or defy the will of the people for they are the true sovereign, the actual depository of power and authority. By their consent and blessings, their leaders rule and govern. If they say to you, with reason, sit down or step down, you comply demurely. And now to you my fellow Liberians:

Stop this sycophancy, duplicity and double-dealing. Refrain from those deceitful resolutions, multiple "Whereas" and useless demonstrations, unbridled acts of corruption, vain glories and divisive tactics. Be men, with spirit or spines, backbones, and not invertebrates. Speak out, stand firm, don't vacilitate, trust in God and do the right things. And all shall be well with you.

FAREWELL! FAREWELL! and FAREWELL!

WHY TARGET NIMBA?

NIMBA COUNTY is located on the northeast of Liberia, bounded by the Republic of the Ivory Coast on the East, the Republic of Guinea on the north, the St. John River on the Southwest, Grand Geddeh County on the East and Grand Bassa County on the South. It is the second largest county in the Republic of Liberia. She was named in honor of the Nimba Mountain which is also located on the north of the county.

This part of Liberia consists of two specific original tribal ethnic groups, the Gio on the southeast and the Mano on the north and southwest. According to studies, both tribes are inter-related through marriages and culture. According to the original history of these people, the Mano tribe migrated from the Republic of Guinea while the Gio tribe also migrated from the French Republic of Ivory Coast. This county is known for its great production in Iron Ore from the Nimba Mountain. This work is done by the J. V. Operating Company—LAMCO. This county is very important in the economic system of the nation. Once upon a time, 95% of the nation's population was employed by this company.

The targeting of Nimba started with the late George Dumbar in the early 1940's and in the late 50's. You may want to go back 55 years or more with me to trace the truth of Liberian leaders targeting the Eastern region. The interior parts of Liberia have always been considered less important or inferior to the urban or coastal areas.

Frankly, Nimba and perhaps Grand Geddeh Counties have been the worst of all; probably, because of their geographic location and subcultures. But, however, a good leader should not use these natural and unavoidable little things to target any society. Especially so when it is a political subdivision of a country of which he claims to be a leader. History tells us that one Mr. George Dumbar used Nimbalians to carry 50 1b. bags of salt on their heads and shoulders from the city of Monrovia to his city, Sanniquellie.

Monrovia City is approximately 350 miles away from Sanniquellie, Nimba County. Intending to create his own salt water in the hinterland, he was the only outstanding leader in the area at the time. Mr. Dumbar would do anything he pleased. He made Nimbalians build roads in the city of Sanniquellie with sticks, no yellow machines or common tools. No modern instruments; such as solvers, wheelbarrows, nothing. After which he bought a pick-up truck and forced Nimbalians to carry it to Nimba County from Monrovia on their heads. These inhumane attitudes led the citizens of Nimba County to become very resistant and aggressive.

Let me take you on a trip to take a look at some aspects of life which Sociology talks about. Then, we will take a very real look at the causes of poverty and the effect therefrom.

Causes of poverty: (1), Economic factors; (2), Discrimination factors, (3), Cultural factors and (4), Political factors. Poverty has no single cause. It is produced by a number of interrelated factors.

Economic Factors

Poverty is usually associated with a lack of jobs. The high unemployment rates found in specific geographic areas and specific sectors of the economy are usually the result of structural changes in economic life, small farmers and agriculture laborers, for example, have been steadily displaced over the years, particularly in Liberia, where one is only able to see subsistence farming methods. In the past few decades, by far, mechanical agriculture and other new methods are nowadays seen; they no longer earn a decent living on the land. Automation in many industries has displaced unskilled workers, but these workers lack the training that would enable them to compete for jobs in industries using advanced technologies. Many workers are trapped in the less skilled service industries as shoe shiners, domestic cleaners, dishwashers, or parking lot attendants, if any.

A poor person, if he or she is able to find employment at all, is concentrated in those jobs that offer only low wages and little security.

Discrimination

Given the prevailing patterns of discrimination in other aspects of social and economic life, it is interesting and hardly surprising that poverty is found disproportionately among minority group members and families headed by women everywhere in the world. Nonwhites generally earn less than whites, even when they have similar qualifications, and women generally earn less than men. Nonwhite women suffer from double discrimination on grounds of both race and sex, and more than half the black families headed by women are in poverty. However, although it is a factor, discrimination in employment practices may not be the primary cause of their economic plight. The origins lie deep in the many subtle influences that prevent both women and minorities from acquiring the education, training and experience necessary to qualify them for the position. Therefore, they are hindered from acquiring some positions. In that light, they are discriminated against in many ways.

To eliminate some problems, the national government needs to eradicate these acts of injustice and discrimination in every aspect of national life. In other parts of the world, discrimination exists between white and black people, as well as people of Asian descent.

But in Liberia, discrimination exists among tribes, sections, and sex. One tribe feels superior to another tribe. Men supress women and children, regardless of their standards of education. Children are also discriminated against due to their social backgrounds. In order for these little children to become part of the whole, they must struggle very hard under a different family's name; some might never succeed.

In the African villages, the men eat the best parts of whatever foodstuffs the villagers get. The growing children and their mothers have serious problems getting the best nutrients needed for body building. The quantity of food given to the men is often three times that of both the women and their children.

The women are often kept out of the major decision-making in the African village. They are only informed by their husbands. Women and children are regarded as being subject to orders from the men.

However, as civilization and modernization spread, more changes began to arrive gradually. In other parts of Liberia, women are nowadays participating in major decision-making. Children can now stand and tell parents no to whatever they feel is wrong.

THE SOLUTION
TO OUR PROBLEM

THE RESULT OF positive thinking. Believe in yourself as a wholesome, functioning individual. Always have faith in your abilities whatever you undertake to do. With a humble, reasonable confidence, not power, you can be successful or happy. Most often people's success comes as a result of self-confidence.

The danger of inadequacy is that it interferes with one's attainment of hopes, whereas self-confidence will lead you to self-realization and moreover better achievement. Due to the essence of this emotional and mental attitude imposed on Liberians by the senseless CIVIL CRISIS, this manuscript will be of help to you.

Believe in yourself and release your emotional and mental distress. I do know that the activities which have taken place and are still going on in Liberia have made life miserable by their atrocities. The nasty spirit of the inferiority complex has already started to work on too many Liberians' minds because of the situation. But you need not personally suffer from this spirit; this is a public trouble, not a personal issue.

You can develop faith in yourself confidentially as a Liberian. Because it has happened to many countries and still can happen anywhere in the world, you are discouraged and depressed. You need not be this way. You may have already been asking yourself, why Liberia? We have been tormented by atrocities of all types; but, nevertheless, God is still on our side. Now listen to my warnings as your fellow Liberian, today, about the result of positive thinking; you want to know by asking how can I do positive thinking or even get some faith in myself that this author is talking about?

There are specifically two steps you have to take. Firstly, it is essential to find out the CAUSATIVE AGENT of these exercises which have created an atmosphere of disbelief. This requires truth analysis and it will take some time, and may also require treatment.

However, to pull you through this immediate problem, I shall give you a formula. As you walk through life today, keep repeating this affirmation of faith: "I can do all things through Jesus Christ which strengthen me." Philipians 4:13. Follow this prescription, and things will surely be all right for you.

Subsequently, you will believe that this simple formula does work. You may have a brother or sister, or even a friend, who made "A's" in school while you only made "C's" and you never heard the last of it, so you believed you could never succeed in life as they could. Because they got "A's" and you got only "C's," you reasoned that you were consigned to getting C's all your life. Apparently, you never realized that some of those who failed to get high grades in school have been the greatest successes outside of school. Just because somebody gets an A in college doesn't make him or her the greatest person in the United States or Liberia because maybe their A's will stop when they get their diploma.

Then the fellow who got C's in school will go on later to get the real A's in life. Other neighboring countries might think that Liberia will forever remain down after the Civil War, this is not true. Let's not forget that the by-product of Civil War is always CIVIL RIGHTS. The greatest secret is, let's fill our good, positive minds with faith.

I must tell you that the blows of life, the accumulation of difficulties, the multiplication of problems tend to sap energy and leave you spent and discouraged. Remember, in such a condition, the true status of one's power is often obscured, and a person yields to a discouragement that is not justified by the facts. It is vitally essential to reappraise your personal assets.

Dr. Karl Menninger, the famous psychiatrist, once said, "Attitudes are more important than facts." Any fact facing us, even seemingly hopeless, is not as important as our attitude toward that fact.

When a human being becomes a demon, he or she cannot think positively. Liberia, for the past one hundred forty-eight years of independence, as a member of the family of nations, has never practiced "demonism" openly until President Doe seized power from Mr. William R. Tolbert Jr. in 1980 in a bloody military coup.

The nationwide errors made by Mr. Samuel K. Doe and his collaborators were of great danger to the survival of the Liberian public. This reminds me of Mr. Adolf Hitler of Germany in 1940. Mr. Hitler, having gained power, unthoughtfully took the most cruel, inhumane decision any leader could make: the decision to murder all the Jews in Germany. Mr. Hitler, assuming that all of the economic power rested in the hands of the Jews, started his cruel demonizational attitudes. The murdering of six plus million Jews by Hitler in Germany was never the solution to the problems of Germany. Just as the placing of 13 noble men of Liberia on the pole facing the firing squad immediately following the April 12, 1980 coup was never the solution of the nation's problems; rather, it was an additional problem for the Liberian people.

At which point, the multiplication of the nation's atrocities was created. The question to the Liberian people in this civil war is, who has the power to decide their happiness or unhappiness? Themselves. From the day of creation, God had made a pronouncement: "man is a free moral agent to decide his own destiny." In that everyone has the mental power to decide his personal happiness or unhappiness in this world.

We are responsible for the result of whatever decision we make. I don't believe in defeat. Defeat comes as a result of our own weaknesses, because there is no difficulty you cannot overcome. A wise and philosophical man once said to me, when asked how he overcame his difficulties, "How do I get through a trouble? Well, first, I try to go around it, and if I can't go around it, I try to get under it, and if I can't get under it, I try to go over it and if I can't go over it, I just plow right through it."

One effective method for making one's mind positive in character is to eliminate certain expressions of thought and speech which we may call the "little negatives." The possibility of these little negatives cluttering up the average person's conversation, and while each one is seemingly unimportant in itself, exists; totaling the effect can also condition the mind negatively.

During the regime of the late Samuel K. Doe, I often heard of the little negatives, so-called rumors in Liberia. I was moved by them to analysis. Having done that for six consecutive years which includes part of Mr. Charles G. Taylor's rebel activities, I finally came to the conclusion that failure could possibly result in both eras, because the former leaders of Liberia took for granted the little negatives, which have become big thoughts.

But it must never be forgotten that "mighty oaks from little acorns grow," and if many little negatives clutter up your conversation, they are bound to seep into your mind.

We must learn how to break our worry habit. Worry should never become your master in life. You need not be a victim of it. Worry is just a destructive mental habit. Hence, we can reduce it. Remember, nobody was born with worry; it is acquired. Eliminate abnormal worry by emptying the mind daily of negative things of life. This process is to be done night after night.

This will lead you to personal problem solving. In this process, always conceive God as a partner. Conceive of yourself as living in daily partnership and companionship with Jesus Christ.

Arms can never solve any problem in the world which we live in today; but, Christ alone does.

ECOMOG supporters maintain that human rights form the foundation of the peace process, and that explicit human rights concerns will be addressed once a peace agreement is in place. The president of Interim Government, Amos Sawyer, put it this way, "Human rights is imbedded in the peace process; it is the democratic process . . . But the first step had to be to stop the fighting—to find out what Taylor wanted, to see how to make concessions to get him to stop fighting, and to convince him to bring his claims to the political process. It didn't work, but the basic principle remains disarmament, encampment and elections. Human rights will then fall in line."

There is little reason to believe that human rights guarantees will be integrated into the peace process, at least not at the initiative of ECOWAS. From November 1990 until October 1992, the two years of the fragile truce, the WEST African leaders and the international community had ample opportunity to address past human rights abuses, including protection for the civilian population and accountability for past human rights abuses. Instead, they have created a situation in which the ultimate political solution will be linked to avoiding accountability on all sides, thus perpetuating the atmosphere of impunity which has plagued Liberia for so long. Accordingly, the ECOWAS leaders, with ECOMOG as their instrument, are contributing to the continuing human rights abuses in Liberia. There is no human rights component to the Yamoussoukro IV accord, October 1991.

A series of meetings were held in Yamoussoukro, in the Ivory Coast. The meeting focused on the question of elections, not only election logistics but also the need to disarm all warring factions and to confine them to their bases. Since the issue of accountability for past abuses was never raised by ECOMOG, or the United Nations, those responsible for gross human rights abuses on all sides to the conflict continue to operate with impunity.

The ECOMOG intervention can be separated into three phases; from August to November 1990, the initial intervention that led to a ceasefire; from November 1990 to October 1992, the fragile truce; and from October 1992 to the present, the renewed war.

Since the November 1990 cease-fire, Liberia has been a divided country, with the Interim Government of National Unity (IGNU) governing Monrovia and its environs, backed by ECOMOG, while the NPFL controlled approximately 90 percent of the country. This situation lasted until late August 1992, when the NPFL, ULIMO, another rebel group formed primarily by soldiers from former president Samuel Doe's army, the AFL, attacked the NPFL from neighboring Sierra Leone, and captured two western counties, Bomi and Grand Cape Mount. However, the situation changed dramatically on October 15, 1992, when the NPFL attacked Monrovia, ending two years of an uneasy peace and plunging the country back into war.

Having failed to enforce a peaceful solution to the crisis, ECOMOG has been dragged back into the war, and is considered by many to constitute a warring faction. Its role has changed from peacekeeping to peace enforcing, and its rules of engagement now are more aggressive—they not only can use force if they feel threatened and are empowered to disarm the warring factions, but they can also attack targets that might contribute to a threat against them.

According to ECOMOG Field Commander Maj. General Adetunji Olurin, a peace-keeping force is supposed to act as an impartial arbiter. However, he explained that they were compelled to change their role into peace enforcement.

If a faction decides to take us on and challenge the peace-keepers, then the enforcement role comes in. We must make all factions comply with the collective wisdom of others—ECOWAS, the OAU or the U.N. One faction cannot be an obstacle to peace. Then, we will return to our peace-keeping posture.

This new role is substantially different from that of a peace-keeper, since it involves aggressive, military operations directed against only one of the parties to the conflict. ECOMOG's actions raise serious questions about the role of a peace-keeping force, and whether its offensive will preclude it from returning to its prior peace-keeping functions.

The only lasting solution to the Liberian crisis will have to be political, based on respect for human rights; the crisis cannot be solved militarily. Since the beginning of the conflict, ECOMOG and ECOWAS have avoided inserting human rights into the peace negotiations, ostensibly for fear of derailing the process; peace, therefore, has been separated from human rights. This is underscored by the alliance ECOMOG has formed since October 1992 with two other Liberian factions—ULIMO and the AFL—whose human rights records range from suspect to abysmal. This, in turn, raises questions about ECOMOG's commitment to human rights, and about the role that human rights should play in the peace process.

According to Africa Watch on Liberia, "Waging War to keep the Peace" the ECOMOG intervention and human rights; in an attempt to end the bloody civil war in Liberia, in August 1990, a group of West African nations under the auspices of the Economic Community of West African States (ECOWAS) took the unprecedented steps of sending a Peace-keeping force into the city of Monrovia. This force, known as the Economic Community Cease-Fire Monitoring Group (ECOMOG), has now spent almost three years in Liberia, yet its goal of bringing peace to the country remains elusive.

The ECOMOG intervention succeeded in temporarily stopping the bloodshed and ethnic killing, and is therefore regarded by many as a model of regional conflict resolution. However, ECOMOG did not integrate human rights protection and promotion into its activities, and this did prove to be a serious shortcoming. Pursuing peace without recognizing the centrality of human rights has left ECOMOG embroiled in a conflict with few immediate prospects for resolution. In the interests of ending the war and defeating a seemingly intractable adversary in Charles Taylor's National Patriotic Front of Liberia (NPFL), ECOMOG has allied itself with other warring factions, which undermines its creditability and therefore its ability to bring peace.

This report evaluates the ECOMOG intervention from a human rights standpoint, with particular emphasis on the period of renewed warfare since October 1992. It does not assess the human rights violations by all sides to the conflict, which has been done in previous Africa Watch Publications; nevertheless, Africa Watch acknowledges that the human rights abuses and intransigent attitude of Charles Taylor's NPFL have constituted a serious obstacle to ECOMOG's efforts. The report concludes that:

The ECOMOG intervention was carried out within clearly stated human rights principles and goals. Although not a part of ECOMOG's mandate, concrete human rights improvements resulted once ECOMOG secured control of Monrovia and its environs in autumn 1990, including a halt to the ethnic-based killing and brutality, the removal of obstacles to the delivery of relief supplies and the re-emergence of civil society.

Since the NPFL attacked Monrovia in October 1992, ECOMOG has unofficially aligned itself with two of the warring factions, the Armed Forces of Liberia (AFL) and the United Liberation Movement for Democracy in Liberia (ULIMO), which are themselves responsible for serious human rights abuses. This has raised questions about ECOMOG's commitment to human rights as well as its ability to act as a neutral arbiter of the conflict. ECOWAS was formed in 1975 and includes 16 West African nations. The ECOWAS charter deals primarily with economic integration and cooperation.

The report is based in part on a fact-finding mission to Liberia and the Ivory Coast in February-March 1993 by Janet Fleischman, research associate for Africa Watch. The names of those interviewed have been withheld upon their request.

Human Rights abuses by the Liberian Peace Council and the need for International Oversight. In late 1993, a new armed faction emerged in Liberia, known as the Liberian Peace Council Southeast of the country. While both sides have been responsible for several human rights abuses against the civilian population, in recent weeks the LPC appears to have stepped up its campaign against civilians, especially those it considers to have supported the NPFL. Some 40,000 civilians have been displaced by the fighting and they describe systematic and gratuitous abuses by the LPC.

There are consistent reports that elements of the Nigerian contingent of ECOMOG, the West African peace-keeping force—not the Ghanaians or the Ugandans, who are also stationed in the area—are aiding the LPC. Displaced persons and other observers report that the Nigerians are supplying arms and ammunition to the LPC as a way to weaken the NPFL, while profiteering on the side. It is not clear how high up the collaboration goes in the Nigeria contingent.

ECOMOG has not sought adequately to count the abusive behavior of the forces with which it is nominally allied or to investigate cases of human rights abuses committed by these forces including killings, beatings, systematic looting and harassment of civilians.

There have been many reports about ECOMOG involvement in looting and occasional harassment or detention of civilians, although ECOMOG has not been responsible for systematic human rights abuses in the territory it controls. However, there is serious concern about the civilian toll and violations of medical neutrality by ECOMOG's air strikes in NPFL territory. There is no indication that ECOMOG has conducted investigations into these incidents.

None of the ECOWAS-sponsored peace talks included human rights on the agenda, thus making the West African countries complicit in the absence of any discussion of human rights protections or accountability for past abuses.

As war factions shatter, Liberia falls into chaos. According to Howard W. French, special correspondent to the New York Times, from the smashed huts strung out along the main roads to the once-imposing buildings like the International Intercontinental Hotel, which long ago became the domain of regular squatters, five years of civil war has left little in Liberia untouched by fighting.

As it has dragged on, what began as a civil war aimed at bringing down a dictator has instead become a free-wheeling struggle that is confusing even to its various ethnically based factions.

Land is claimed but rarely held for long. Fighting is financed by pillaging and plunder. And neither combatants nor civilians enjoy even the minimal protections accorded in conflicts elsewhere.

As a result, Liberia has come to bear little resemblance to a modern state, becoming instead a tribal cauldron governed less by commonly understood rules than at any time since it became Africa's first republic in 1847 under freed American slaves.

"Things have deteriorated to the point where what we are seeing emerge nowadays are sub-warlords, each of whom is a law unto himself," said Amos Sawyer, an author of Liberia's Constitution. He served as interim President but resigned in March when militias refused to respect an agreement to disarm.

"If we don't arrest the situation quickly," Mr. Sawyer continued, "We will soon be back to where we were. Warlords have refused to disarm more than a token number of fighters and elections due to have been held this week are indefinitely postponed at the time again."

Aid agencies in Liberia on Thursday of that week reported a sharp rise in violence and appealed to warring factions to respect the neutrality of their staff. Contrary to earlier reports, two smaller militias, the Liberia Peace Council (LPC) and Lofa Defense Force (LDF), were not invited to Akosombo and were not represented.

Alhaji Kromah took the ULIMO seat even though the militia is now split on tribal lines between his Mandingoes and Roosevelt Johnson's Krahn.

Now the opposition to the Liberian Peace Treaty waning comes in; in Monrovia, September 27, 1994, (Reuters)—Liberian politicians who vigorously opposed the country's latest peace treaty at birth two weeks ago, showed signs of moving towards acceptance of the accord on Monday when they called for its amendment rather than its destruction.

A month old national conference in the capital voted to "receive subject to further discussion" a report by conference chairman Junius Baryounger recommending changes to the treaty which he initially condemned as ushering in military rule.

The accord signed in the Ghanaian town/city of Akosombo, gave the country's three main militias—the National Patriotic Front of Liberia (NPFL), the Armed Forces of Liberia (AFL), and ULIMO—a seat each on a five-member collective presidency, called the Council of State. A fourth would be allocated jointly by the NPFL and ULIMO and the fifth member named by the conference, the treaty said. Baryounger said smaller militias, two of them linked to the AFL through prior service and Krahn tribal ties, should have a say in choosing the AFL presidential delegate.

It is acceptable that the said NPFL and ULIMO should maintain their one representative each. However, instead of the AFL being the entity to name their representative, their representative should be nominated by the military coalition forces which encompass the AFL, ULIMO, LPC and the LDF, he said.

His reference to ULIMO was interpreted as meaning a breakaway Krahn wing of the militia which has taken a major part in recent fighting at the time.

He also proposed cutting the 16-month transition period enshrined in the Akosombo accord, but did not say by how much.

A recommendation to delay transfer of power to the new council until disarmament of at least 25 percent of the faction fighters was seen by local officials and foreign analysts as sure to lead to more delays in ending nearly five years of civil war if accepted by the conference. It's 25 percent of what? You have some estimates saying there are 30,000 fighters out there and others saying 40,000 or 60,000. How do you verify it? They are going to be talking this one out for a long time, an analyst said.

The Akosombo treaty has already fallen behind its own timetable. Council members were to have been named by September 19 and sworn in by September 26. Neither has so far happened. Nor seems likely to in the coming days.

The initial blazing hostility to the United Nations backed back to the capital and telephone lines to most places down since the December 1989 outbreak of war, there is no independent confirmation or denial of conflicting claims by militia heads to be in control of Gbarnga.

Taylor, speaking by satellite telephone to BBC radio on Monday, said he was on the edge of Gbarnga, fighting to regain his heavily-fortified command centre, Government officials doubted he was anywhere near the city.

"It's a no-man's land. Even people supposed to be helping each other are killing each other by mistake. There is a lot of dying being done up there and no way Taylor is going to get too close until it stabilizes," an official said.

According to one reporter, Stanton Peabody, Monrovia, September 21 (Reuters)—Liberian Labour Minister Tom Woewiyu says 1,000 fighters loyal to his former leader, Charles Taylor, have surrendered to a coalition of rival militias who have overrun Taylor's inland stronghold in the town of Gbarnga.

Woewiyu, a leader of a breakaway wing of Taylor's National Patriotic Front of Liberia (NPFL), told reporters on Tuesday that the loyalists would be handed over to ECOMOG African troops in Kakata, northeast of Monrovia on the road to Gbarnga.

"They are being evacuated under coalition escort to ECOMOG positions in Kakata where they will be safely kept," he said. Woewiyu was appointed by Taylor to represent the NPFL in a transitional coalition government but turned against his leader almost as soon as he took up his post. Taylor has ordered him replaced but he shows no sign of giving up his position.

He was speaking from the capital and is now known to have visited Gbarnga, 100 miles (160 kilometers) away.

ECOMOG confirmed the surrender. "They have been turned over to our headquarters in Kakata," an officer told Reuters. Fighting is reported continuing in Gbarnga, where Woewiyu said he was in alliance with ULIMO and the smaller Liberia Peace Council (LPC) and Lofa Defense Force (LDF) militias. He made no mention of the Armed Forces of Liberia (AFL) which took part in an earlier attack against Gbarnga but has since been shaken by a coup attempt from within its ranks and a row over a peace accord marrying the AFL to ULIMO and Taylor.

ULIMO too has a breakaway wing, of Krahn tribesmen, which attacked an ECOMOG convoy in Kakata on September 14 killing at least two Tanzanian soldiers. ECOMOG says four are missing. An aide to Krahn ULIMO leader General Roosevelt Johnson told Reuters his men were in possession of Tanzanian passports in the names of David Kuyeja Salamani, David Nwallulu Mbosso, Khalifa Ali Naaibu and Adamu Ali Kwartay. He could not say if the two dead were among those named.

"The attack came as a complete shock; we were all very certain that we had made it", said Juerg Frei, one of six foreign relief workers in Gbarnga traveling with the 25-vehicle convoy. Frei, who had high praise for the Tanzanian troops, said the convey finally made it to Monrovia on September 17.

On the way from Gbarnga Frei, a 34-year-old Swiss working as a field delegate for the International Committee of the Red Cross, said the convoy passed at least 20 roadblocks manned by different militias. Many of the fighters were drugged and some were small boys no taller than their rifles. "We saw one at a roadblock. The man had been disembowelled and his intestines used as a string across the road," Frei said in Abidjan on his way back to Switzerland.

"There is no respect for civilians whatsoever. The people are completely at the mercy of the moods of whoever is carrying a gun," he said. ECOMOG was sent to Liberia by the Economic Community of West Africa States (ECOWAS) in 1990 in an attempt to end the civil war launched by Taylor in December 1989.

Civilian politicians and the militia delegates started a second day of talks in Ghana on Wednesday in an attempt to patch up the September 12 treaty, which already shows signs of collapsing under the weight of continued fighting and civilian opposition to provisions giving political power to the big three. Mainstream leader, Alhaji Kroma, attending the talks, downplayed battles raging in central and southeastern Liberia. Although fighting is going on in some parts of the country, it is not so intense as to derail the peace process as it has been said by some.

Chaos continued in Liberia after accord, eleven of the observers exclaimed. In Monrovia on September 14, Liberia slid deeper into chaos on Wednesday, despite a new peace treaty; with reports of widespread fighting, a flight of refugees and the U.N. appealing for the release of observers and aid workers it said were held by rebels. Accordingly, eleven of the 43 U.N. observers were freed on Wednesday and crossed to safety in Ivory Coast, one of the officers said.

Much of the combat was around and in the central town of Gbarnga, headquarters of Charles Taylor's National Patriotic Front of Liberia (NPFL) and where government radio reported street fighting between NPFL renegades and Taylor loyalists. Both sides have claimed victory, as has the ULIMO militia which has been attacking Gbarnga in an alliance with the Armed Forces of Liberia AFL and smaller groups for three weeks at the time, but no independent source could say for sure who was in control.

The commander of the 160-strong U.N. military observers' mission in Liberia, General Daniel Opande appealed for the release of 43 of his men he said were being held hostage around Gbarnga and in the south and east, where fighting has intensified.

"I would like to appeal to anybody of those factions that are holding our military observers, they should realize the military observers are not part and parcel of this conflict," he told British Broadcasting Corporation radio.

"They should be treated without intimidation; they should be released immediately," he added. As Opande spoke, 11 of his unarmed observers crossed into the Ivory Coast from a Taylor-held part of Liberia. "There was some mistreatment, but we were not beaten up. Some of our things were taken," one officer, who declined to give his identity, told Reuters by telephone from the border town of Danane, Ivory Coast.

Those freed were from Uruguay, India, the Czech Republic, Austria, Slovakia, China and Guinea Bassau, he said. He expected other observers to be released soon but was not sure which militias were holding them.

The United Nations Security Council on Tuesday strongly condemned the detention of its observers, who it said were being mistreated. A spokesman at the United Nations New York headquarters said that they were held by the NPFL renegades. A statement from the United Nations in Monrovia said six aid workers were also being held.

But 11 were held in three factions locations still controlled by Taylor loyalists. They met Taylor on a Wednesday morning at Sanniquellie in his shrinking enclave. Aid officers said there that more than 100 Tanzanian peace troops based on the outskirts of Gbarnga had been authorized to pull back towards Monrovia, but fighting on the road may have prevented them from moving out.

They said at least 40,000 frightened civilians from Gbarnga and towns further north had fled into Guinea, while in the southeast 3,000 refugees fleeing fighting around the part of Harper had crossed into neighboring Ivory Coast.

The NPFL, ULIMO and AFL signed a peace accord on Monday, after declaring an immediate halt to fighting which has plagued the country since civil war broke out in December 1989. Analysts' skepticism that the treaty would fare any better than previous agreements appeared to be borne out by the continued fighting.

Taylor flew to Ivory Coast on Tuesday after pledging to return to Gbarnga, which he said was under his control. He later crossed the border, but aid officials monitoring the unrest said he would not be able to cover the 106 miles (170 km) to Gbarnga easily or quickly, if, at all, and would have to fight much of the way.

Fierce Battle Reported at Taylor's NPFL Headquarters

Monrovia, 11th September: A fierce battle raged Sunday (11th September) in northeast Liberia between supporters and adversaries of Charles Taylor, leader of the National Patriotic Front of Liberia (NPFL), for control of the movement's headquarters, informed sources said.

The sources, who requested anonymity, said forces loyal to Taylor were still managing to hold out at the NPFL stronghold of Gbarnga against an assault by dissidents from within their own movement and forces from one of the NPFL's rivals, the United Liberation Movement (for Democracy in Liberia) (ULIMO). ULIMO itself is divided into two rival Krahn and Mandingo branches. The sources reported "heavy gunfire" in Gbarnga, 160 km (100 miles) northeast of Monrovia, but were unable to give details of casualties. Most civilians were believed to have fled the area.

NPFL-run radio, which normally broadcasts from the town, went off the air on Wednesday (7th September). Taylor, himself, was still in Ghana Sunday at multiparty talks aimed at thrashing out a new 10-point peace agreement to put an end to almost five years of civil war in Liberia. Late Saturday, he had said his forces had managed to repel the dissident revolt at Gbarnga.

According to reports reaching AFP, Gbarnga forces loyal to Taylor have been placed under the command of his head of security General Cassius Jacobs. That group is faced by an unknown number of men led by General Samuel Varney. Varney was formerly the right-hand man of Prince Johnson, a lieutenant of Taylor when the conflict broke out in December 1989. Six months later, Johnson left to form the dissident Independent National Patriotic Front of Liberia.

When the NPFL launched an assault on Monrovia, Johnson sought protection from the Economic Community of West African States (ECOWAS), which sent peace-keeping troops to the war-torn country in August 1990. He then left for Lagos, where he is believed still to be based, while his supporters rejoined the NPFL.

Taylor and Liberia's other warring faction chiefs were meanwhile still aboard a yacht off Ghana on Sunday hoping to have a peace accord ready for Tuesday (13th September), a Ghanaian source said.

The source said a draft accord provided for the revision of the mandate, composition, mode of appointment and the functioning of a transitional presidency, government and parliament set up in Monrovia in March last year under the 1993 Cotonou agreement.

Ghana Tells Liberians to Order Ceasefire

In Akosombo, Ghana, September 9, Ghana, hosting Liberian peace talks, told warlords on Friday to order an immediate ceasefire and end renewed fighting.

Ghana's President, Mr. Jerry Rawlings, convened the talks to try to prevent a full-scale resumption of the five year civil war.

A Ghana government statement confirmed heavy fighting around Ghana, the inland capital of Liberia's main militia leader, Charles Taylor.

"Ghana regrets that while leaders of Liberia's warring parties are engaged in talks aimed at finding a durable solution to the Liberian civil war, fighting appears to have intensified around Gbarnga and other areas. Ghana calls on leaders of warring parties to order their forces to lay down their arms and observe an immediate cease-fire," the statement said. It was issued on the third day of a peace conference at Akosombo, 100 kms (65 miles) from Accra, the Ghanaian capital.

There was no immediate response to the cease-fire call from Taylor and the other main militia chiefs at the talks, Alhaji Kromah of ULIMO and General Hezekiah Bowen of the Armed Forces of Liberia (AFL). Alhaji Kromah took the ULIMO seat even though the militia is now split along tribal lines between the Mandingos and Roosevelt Johnson's Krahn. Contrary to earlier reports, two smaller militias, the Liberia Peace Council (LPC) and the Lofa Defense Force (LDF) were not invited to Akosombo and were not represented.

"The warring factions were said on Friday to be mapping out a revised version of their failed 1993 peace accord. The aim of the closed session today is to remove misunderstandings before what we hope will be a final plenary session on Saturday" one Ghanaian official said. The fighting around Taylor-controlled Gbarnga and Ganta broke out on Monday, shortly after Taylor's 63-member delegation left for Ghana.

It was unclear if the clashes were caused by a power struggle between rival groups in Taylor's National Patriotic Front of Liberia (NPFL) or were due to an attack by a coalition of enemy militias. The latest fighting comes after months of low-level conflict between militias in several areas of the devastated West African country.

Warlords have refused to disarm more than a token number of fighters and elections due to have been held this week are indefinitely postponed.

Aid agencies in Liberia on Thursday reported a sharp rise in violence and appealed to warring factions to respect the neutrality of their staff.

"People in Liberia are not very analytical, they are easily fooled and they were whipped up over this by people who wanted to safeguard their jobs in the existing system," one said. "There was a serious failure by the United Nations to sell Akosombo to the Liberian people. If the opposition is now easing, it's because information is coming through and people see it is really not such a departure from the (1993) Cotonou treaty," a Monrovia-based political analyst said.

Fighting was reported continuing regardless of the status of the peace talks, but little detail has emerged. Most of the bloodshed was around the central town of Gbarnga and the southeastern port of Harper, aid workers said.

Gbarnga was the central point or capital of NPFL chief Mr. Charles G. Taylor until his men were forced out by rival militias and NPFL dissidents at the same time as their leaders were proclaiming peace in Akosombo.

United Nations military observers, of whom 43 were seized by guerrilla fighters and then released into neighboring Ivory Coast or back to Monrovia, have now quit the combat zones and according to one of their officials are unlikely to be replaced. "Our mission is over, there is nothing left to do anymore. We took all the risks but, in the end, we achieved nothing," a weary looking colonel said.

According to the human rights report of February 1, 1991, at the beginning of 1990, Liberia was a nation which, while theoretically under a constitution and legal system patterned on America's, was in essence ruled by one man; Samuel K.Doe, through his army and political party. In late December 1989, a small group of insurgents from the National Patriotic Front of Liberia (NPFL), led by Charles G. Taylor, crossed into Liberia from the Ivory Coast to attack government targets in northeastern Liberia (Nimba County). The Armed Forces of Liberia (AFL) responded by carrying out a brutal series of attacks on civilian targets in Nimba, singling out members of the Mano and Gio tribes for retribution because of their perceived support for the rebels.

The Gio and Mano responded by siding with the insurgents and targetting Doe's tribe (the Krahn), along with the Mandingo, whose role as small merchants made them unpopular, and many of whom were perceived as supporting the government. The insurgency spread throughout Liberia, but, although NPFL forces reached the suburbs of Monrovia in early June, they were unable to defeat the AFL. By early July, all semblance of the old government's authority had vanished, leaving a stalemate in which various military commanders wielded de facto executive and judicial power in their respective areas of control. Eventually, the NPFL was driven back by a five-nation West African Peacekeeping force (ECOMOG), which entered Monrovia at the end of August, and a splinter rebel group, the Independent National Patriotic Front of Liberia (INPFL), led by former Taylor military commander Prince Johnson, an "Interim Government of National Unity."

Human Rights Report

According to the human rights report of February, 1992, throughout 1991 Liberia remained a nation divided into two parts and three armed camps as a result of the war. The Interim Government of National Unity (IGNU), headed by President Amos Sawyer, represented a broad range of political views, but it exercised administration over only Monrovia and its immediate environs.

About 50% of the total population in Liberia resided in this area which is totally within the defensive perimeter of the Economic Community of West African States (ECOWAS) which served as the ceasefire monitoring group (ECOMOG). The National Patriotic Reconstruction Assembly Government (NPRAG), based on and supported by the National Patriotic Forces of Liberia (NPFL), led by Charles G. Taylor, exercised political sway throughout the remaining ninety percent of the country.

The two other former warring parties, the Independent National Patriotic Front of Liberia (INPFL), led by Prince Y. Johnson, and the Armed Forces of Liberia (AFL) were encamped in Monrovia. Both INPFL and AFL factions, while monitored by ECOMOG, retained arms within their respective camps and the INPFL sometimes acted independently. Johnson, on several occasions, killed a number of people, most of them members of his force.

It can be recorded that the economy, based primarily on iron ore, rubber, and timber, was ravaged by the civil war. Gross domestic product for 1991 was no more than 25 percent of pre-war levels. The United States and other Western relief agencies and non-governmental organizations initiated massive emergency operations in late 1990 to prevent widespread starvation in both parts of the country. These operations continued through 1991.

When compared to the appalling civil war conditions of 1990, one would possibly say that there was some improvement in the human rights situation in 1991, especially in the city of Monrovia, an area controlled by ECOMOG forces. However, the Interim Government's authority was limited, and all Liberian military forces committed serious human rights violations in 1991, including summary executions. The NPFL, in particular, detained several thousand West Africans throughout much of 1991, and NPFL soldiers reportedly killed many Krahn residents of Grand Gedeh in mid year.

To assist ECOMOG and the civilians in Monrovia, a police force was begun and only constituted in 1991. It was only in Monrovia, and most of them remained unarmed. ECOMOG assumed this function to a large extent in Monrovia. The NPFL policed the territory under its control, and, to a large extent, both the INPFL and AFL carried out this function within their camps. Soldiers from the warring factions regularly abused their position by mistreating civilians, usually in attempts to extort money and goods.

Despite the continuing unstable security situation, there was some hope at year's end for a political solution following peace initiatives conducted by West African nations which led to general agreement on the need for free, internationally supervised elections in 1992. Implementation of the agreements is not assured. At the end of 1991, it was estimated that as many as twenty thousand to thirty thousand Liberians may have died in the conflict and approximately 600,000 more were refugees in neighboring countries.

The doubt continues to ring on people's minds for human rights. Respect for human rights, respect for the integrity of the person, including freedom from political and other extra-judicial killing.

In spite of all efforts to restore human rights protections in Liberia at the time, indiscriminate killings did not stop. However, after awhile, indiscriminate killings declined sharply from the previous year, although many incidents continued to be reported (see section 1g). Prince Johnson, the leader of the INPFL, was believed responsible for the killing in July of several soldiers of his own movement, including senior commando Moses Varney. The INPFL leader maintained that the soldiers had been tripled under internal procedures and executed when found guilty. No details of the trials were made public. The IGNU condemned the killings. Johnson was also reportedly responsible for killing some civilians in September, but no action was taken against him as a consequence.

According to the Liberian religious leaders, NPFL soldiers were also responsible for killing twenty Ghanaians in Sinoe County in mid February, and in July several Ghanaian women from Fanti fishing communities informed an international organization's representatives in Cote d'Ivoire that the NPFL had killed their husbands. These reported killings continued a pattern from the previous year when NPFL followers allegedly killed Ghanaians and other West Africans in retribution for their respective nations' role in the conflict.

NPFL leader Charles Taylor reportedly ordered several NPFL members executed following an aborted coup attempt in late August while Taylor publicly denied there had been a coup attempt. He acknowledged that an NPFL officer had been executed, ostensibly for killing five NPFL soldiers. According to Monrovia's media, which claimed to have intervewed ex-NPFL soldiers following the failed coup, up to seventyfive NPFL soldiers (members) were executed.

Disappearance

Disappearances were much less common in 1991, but little new information surfaced about persons missing as a result of the war. Many families remained divided among those living in Monrovia, those in NPFL areas, and those who fled Liberia and have not returned. Although there were many returnees during the year, movement between Monrovia and the NPFL areas was very difficult for most people.

The International Committee of the Red Cross (ICRC) began a family tracer program but located only about thirty percent of the missing persons brought to its attention. According to a Liberian religious leader, several Ghanaian children disappeared in March in Buchanan following a visit by ECOMOG intended to build confidence between itself and the NPFL. Ghanaian children warmly welcomed ECOMOG vehicles, some manned by Ghanaian soldiers. This affectionate display was said to have enraged some NPFL soldiers who were believed responsible for the children's disappearance shortly thereafter.

According to a human rights report, February 19, 1992, during the height of the civil-war, many members of the three warring factions rampantly indulged in acts of inhumanity. Abuses in 1991 declined sharply, but cases of inhuman treatment continued. The most widely publicized incident occurred in February when INPFL forces inflicted inhuman treatment on nine members of the IGNU, including a cabinet minister-designate and several members of the IGNU Interim Legislative Assembly.

They were stripped and flogged, and one was forced to sit in a mound of driver ants while another was made to lick feces. Under pressure from ECOMOG, the ICRC, and the Interim Government, INPFL Leader Johnson released the detainees, excusing his actions as necessary to call attention to alleged ECOMOG abuse of INPFL soldiers.

Prior to the 1989 civil war, conditions in the nation's jails were inhuman and hazardous to life and health. Prisoners were often denied access to family and medical care, cells were small, crowded, and filthy. Conditions at the notorious maximum security at Belle Yella Prison had long been of concern.

During 1991, none of Liberia's prewar prisons were believed to be still functioning, although the IGNU was reported to be reburbishing one in Monrovia. NPFL Leader Charles Taylor announced in March that the Belle Yella Prison would be closed. He directed that its remaining prisoners be transferred to their respective counties for retrial. There was no information about the results of the transfer order.

Human Rights Report, 1994

According to a human rights report in 1994, Liberia remained a country increasingly divided factionally, even though warring factions did conclude an agreement in late December on ending the country's civil war. The

Liberian National Transitional Government (LNTG) was seated after much delay in March as the successor to the Interim Government of National Unity (IGNU), which along with the National Patriotic Front of Liberia (NPFL) and the United Liberation Movement for Democracy in Liberia (ULIMO) signed the July 1993 Cotonou Peace Agreement under the aegis of the Economic Community of West African States (ECOWAS), the United Nations, and the Organization of African Unity.

The Cotonou Accord did not, however, resolve the basic factional differences over political power or lead to the project demobilization of the warring factions, or to plan free elections. In fact, the three groups that signed the Accord mushroomed to seven competing political-military groups which renewed factional fighting, thereby preventing the LNTG from extending its authority outside greater Monrovia and the corridor to Buchanan. Throughout much of the year, the shifting factional military action served to keep Charles Taylor's NPFL forces, which almost captured Monrovia in late 1992, on the defensive.

As one may note in the confusing Liberian mosaic of political/military forces, an eighth group, composed of civilian political parties and other interest groups, convened a National Conference in August to pressure the armed factions to disarm and implement other Cotonou Accord provisions. The Conferences strongly opposed a new agreement reached on September 12 in Akosombo, Ghana, by the Cotonou signatories, including the Armed Forces of Liberia (AFL) replacing the dissolved IGNU, under the auspices of ECOWAS Chairman Ghanaian President Jerry Rawlings. The Conference participants insisted that the new accord excessively favored warring faction interests. While fighting raged in Liberia between followers of the faction leaders meeting in Ghana, Mr. Rawlings continued to consult with the various Liberian parties, including the National Conference.

According to the United States, State Department, on 15 March, their leaders signed the Akosombo Clarification Agreement (three parties) and the Agreement of Acceptance and Accession (five parties, including the National Conference) on December 21 in Accra. The Accra Accords provided for a cease-fire on December 28 and established a 5-member ruling Council to be inaugurated in early 1995 to govern the country, including conducting the November 1995 elections, until an elected government takes over in January 1996.